BE A
SHORTCUT

BE A SHORTCUT

The Secret Fast Track to Business Success

SCOTT G. HALFORD

WILEY

John Wiley & Sons, Inc.

Published by John Wiley & Sons, Inc., Hoboken, New Jersey.
Published simultaneously in Canada.

For general information on our other products and services or for technical support, please contact
our Customer Care Department within the United States at (800) 762-2974, outside the United
States at (317) 572-3993 or fax (317) 572-4002.

Wiley also publishes its books in a variety of electronic formats. Some content that appears in print
may not be available in electronic books. For more information about Wiley products, visit our web
site at www.wiley.com.

Library of Congress Cataloging-in-Publication Data:

Halford, Scott G., 1960-
 Be a shortcut : the secret fast-track to business success / Scott G. Halford.
  p. cm.
 Includes bibliographical references and index.
 ISBN 978-0-470-27036-3 (cloth)
  1. Success in business. I. Title.
 HF5386.H223 2009
 650.1—dc22

2008022838

Printed in the United States of America

10 9 8 7 6 5 4 3 2 1

To all who make the journey easier and sweeter.

Contents

Acknowledgments   xi

Preface   xv

Introduction   xxi

Shortcut Quiz   xxiii

Part One   The Know-Why   1

Back-Road Basics   7
If You're Not a Shortcut You're Taking Up Too Much Space   11
Are You a Shortcut or Bottleneck?   16
Determining Your Value   18
Anatomy of a Bottleneck   27
Shortcuts Save Time   29

Part Two   The Know-What   35

Make It Easier, Make It Better, Make More Money   37
The Shortcut of Efficiency (Easier)   41
Organize Your Info   44
Unload the Overload   47
Scoop It Up   51
The Washed-Up Shortcut   53
Raise Your Hand   55
Get Some Screen Time   58
Rule the Rules   61

Become the Master   65
Find the Flow   74
Train Your Brain   81
Incite Your Insights   89
Throw Some Spice on the Grill   96
Use the White Space   98
Excel as a White Belt First   101
Get Framed   104
Be the Influencer   107

Part Three   The Know-How   115

Image   123
The Care and Feeding of Your Shanti   131
Attitude   139
Emotional Intelligence   144
Focus   153
Meaning   157
Humor: The Secret Weapon of Shortcuts Everywhere   161
"Yes": Why It's Usually the Right Answer   163
Choices   167
Stickiness   170
Responsibility   173
Feelings   176
Context   179

Part Four   The Shortcut as a Company   185

Shortcuts Transform   197
Shortcut Paradise   200
Shortcuts Here, There, and Everywhere   202
Shortcuts Remember When . . .   205

Part Five   The Long and Shortcut of It   207

The Lessons of the Shortcut Have Always Been There   211

Epilogue   215

Appendix: Shortcut Quiz Answers   217

References   223

Bibliography   227

About the Author   229

Index   231

Acknowledgments

Writing a book is an amazing process, and many who do it liken it to the birthing of a child. Since I'm a guy, I wouldn't presume to know about that, but I do know that a human infant takes nine months to develop, from conception to seeing the light. This "baby" has been gestating now for about four times that long, and during that period many people stood on the sidelines as if they were watching a marathon, shouting their encouragement, offering a helping hand, and simply giving me the confidence to help me across the finish line. Thank you from the deepest part of my soul to all of you who were there. Even the quickest and lightest touch along the way was enough to encourage me to take one more step.

There is no Shortcut to thanking the people who made this massive undertaking come together. But as my thank-you list would take as many pages as this book, I ask those I don't name by name to forgive me. I assure you, your spirit and lessons are in this book, and I hope you recognize that as the greatest gift you could give.

To Maddy Breeden, thank you for being my cheerleader on those days when I felt like I wasn't even in the game. Your unwavering support lifts my heart. You make life a wonderful adventure.

To Marty Lassen, my soul mate, encourager, and voice of sanity. You are my Shortcut to so many things.

To the Indigo Ladies, Marci, Sandy and Stacy, thank you for making me look good. You are my backbone, and the reason I can get so much done.

To my dear friend Mary Lo Verde, who looked at the first miserable manuscript a few years ago and said, "You have to do this." Here it is; your magic is in these pages.

To Becky Cabaza: Your head and your heart make mine bigger and better. Thank you for helping me sculpt the thoughts and words; and for giving me gentle but firm nudges to make everything make sense.

To Lou Heckler: You'll find so much of your grey matter in these pages. Brilliance like yours is so rare and so precious because you share it and make us all feel so much smarter.

To Sam Horn, whose name probably appears in so many of the acknowledgment pages of the authors you've nurtured, and whose manuscripts you've helped give life to: Thank you for breathing life into this project, as well.

To Amy Jarrett, my artist and designer extraordinaire: Working with you is like eating my favorite ice cream—always good, always sweet, and always hits the spot.

To Amy Miller: Your insights and suggestions are right-on. How lucky the world is to be graced by your compassion and brilliance in human interaction.

To Laurie Stephenson: You are one of the greatest Shortcuts I've met; and without you, I would never have felt the peace and comfort that you brought to the process. Thank you for your experience and wisdom.

To Cheryl Olson, who diligently transcribed hours of my voice, jabbering on about Shortcuts. Your quick fingers made this work possible.

My deepest gratitude to all the kind and generous people at John Wiley & Sons: Matt Holt for taking a chance, Christine Moore for moving this book from infancy to adulthood, Jessica

Campilango for keeping it all sane and on target, Miriam Palmer-Sherman for getting it out the door, Janice Borzendowski for making me look like I actually understand the English language, and Christine Kim for causing my heart to leap with excitement when I saw the first book covers. You are all Shortcuts to dreams; and the beauty is, you don't even know it.

To Moose and Big Blue: I love you both for what you taught me throughout life. You're the greatest Shortcuts of all.

Preface

What a Shortcut Looks Like: The Rescuer on the River of Life

There is no better way to thank God for your sight than by giving a helping hand to someone in the dark.

—HELEN KELLER
American educator and author, 1880–1968

Early one summer, I was white-water rafting down the Arkansas River in the Royal Gorge Canyon of Colorado when the water was extremely high and swift. At the midpoint of our journey, the guides had to decide whether or not to close the river because the rapids were swelling above the level that even advanced rafters could navigate. They chose not to close the river, instead selecting only two of the eight boats to continue into the most difficult water. As fate would have it, I was in one of the boats selected.

My fellow rafters and I were briefed about what to do to stay afloat and how to react should any of us or the entire raft get tossed. There were rescue kayakers and ropes stretched across the river. I knew that this was an incredibly big deal, and I felt I did not belong there. But I was young and headstrong and with a bunch of guys who all had to prove how cool we were by traveling down this river of insanity.

Our raft flipped within three seconds of entering the Sunshine Falls, a narrow rapid that fell under the 5.5 classification—the most advanced class of rapid before the river is closed to rafting.

If you have ever experienced utter chaos, panic, terror, frustration, and confusion, all at the same time, then you understand what was coursing through my brain in those seconds when I was held beneath the water and literally spewed out near a slippery boulder.

Though closer to dry land, I was still battling the white water to swim frantically toward terra firma when a rescuer yelled for me to clutch the rope strung overhead. When I grabbed it and made my way safely to shore, I remember thinking how "in love" with that rope and rescuer I was. No, I don't think "love" is too strong a word here. They were my lifeline, my buddy, my savior. I actually cried with relief.

I think back on that trip with fondness, because no one was badly hurt. Plus, we all won bragging rights and had a story to tell, one that grew larger than it really was (in the retelling, all of us nearly died, which was a bit of an overstatement). More important, I learned a universal life lesson, which finds its way here in these pages.

The rope and rescuer symbolize to me all that is good and right in a Shortcut—the entire idea behind this book. The rescuer did his job. He was there exactly when I needed him; not a moment before and not a moment too late. He didn't complain about carrying my weight, and he didn't make me feel bad for not doing my part of the job. He wasn't looking to get an "atta boy," or a tip, or to show off. He didn't lament that the guide should have done this or that in order to avoid spilling the raft; he wasn't focused on blame or one-upping. He was there in case we needed him; and when we did, he responded perfectly. I don't know if his "real job" was a kayaker, or a raft guide, or an adventurer on that day—he didn't tell me. What I do know is that he was an expert rescuer who wielded a rope, and that made all the difference in the world to me. It wasn't his aspirations and ambitions that impacted my life, but rather the fact that he was who he was supposed to be on that day and in that moment: a rescuer.

That's a Shortcut—someone who rescues us from drowning in the sea of information and expectations that surround us at work. Shortcuts are there to help us be successful. The Shortcut can be you; and the purpose of this book is to show you why and how to be that person. Whether you work for one boss or for yourself, or you have a whole department full of direct reports or a temp assistant who comes in once a week, you can build Shortcut skills that will make you invaluable to your managers as well as your colleagues, customers, and others who depend upon you and your services. You may run your own business, or you may work for a massive global corporation. No matter where you are in your organization—or what kind of organization you are a part of—you're about to see how you can bring value as a Shortcut, and how you'll be rewarded.

When my buddies and I were all pulled ashore that day of the rafting trip, I remember watching the rescuer wrap the rope tidily around his arm. Strange as it sounds, I felt an oddly deep kinship and gratitude toward someone who simply smiled and said he was just doing his job—and then walked off. If he had asked me for an out-of-the-way ride on my way back to Denver, I would have gladly obliged. All of us would have. In that moment, this bearded, athletic outdoorsman became one of the most influential people in my life. I remember reflecting on the episode several times. Each time I did, I didn't focus on the sheer fear I experienced that day; instead, the memory of my rescuer kept entering into my consciousness. How did he manage to be so effective in such a short amount of time? How could a stranger make me feel adoration and safety beyond what could be expected from falling into a river? Why do I find myself comparing his humble yet awe-inspiring attributes to people in every walk of life? The answer is manyfold; but at its base is the fact that the rescuer's powerful knowledge, concentration, intention, skill—essentially, his entire physical being—was poured into one moment for one person to do one thing: be there for me. It was pretty extraordinary, and fostered a feeling quite unlike any other I have experienced, and I wanted to know how to replicate it. How could I create that same reaction in others?

After my rafting trip, as I watched other people in the world go about their work, I noticed that a select few had the same effect on people as the rescuer had had on me. People talked of their own "rescuers" glowingly. Most would give this person an "out-of-the-way" favor. And then I saw it: the commonality between the Shortcut and the rescuer. The journey you're about to row through in the pages of this book will help you to reflect, learn, and earn the incredible power of the Shortcut. Think back to the rescuer on my rafting journey, and you'll understand what this book is about. Here are some of the things that a Shortcut—like the rescuer—embodies.

Shortcuts

- Are there when you need them.

- Humbly do their jobs so that others can "survive" and thrive in their jobs.

- Don't complain about having to sometimes carry the weight of others.

- Are happy to help make you successful.

- Don't waste time trying to convince you how good they would be doing something else.

- Are experts in their own little corner of the world.

- Don't try to be all things to all people.

- Don't have a sour attitude.

- Don't make you feel indebted to them just because they do their job so excellently for you.

- Have immeasurable influence.

- Are attractors.

- Are smart and know their stuff—and a lot of your stuff, as well.

- Command respect, admiration, even affection from those who use them as a Shortcut.

You can see that most of the Shortcut attributes are about *how* you are, not *what* you are. You'll find that the passage to become a superstar Shortcut—one who is highly valued and influential—is a combination of know-*what* and know-*how*. It's the blend of expertise with emotional intelligence.

In my more than 20 years of being invited to work with employees and their executives around the world to help them master the intricacies of human interaction, the ones who end up most successful and most fulfilled, time and time again, are the Shortcuts. I've worked with Shortcut file clerks, administrators, midlevel managers, executive vice presidents; chief operating, financial, technology, information, and marketing officers; presidents and boards of directors. All of them benefit from and excel in being a Shortcut. Those who don't embrace the Shortcut Way eventually lose their jobs—often in a not-so-elegant takedown.

Most of us are looking for Shortcuts because we don't have the time to deal with all that's coming at us. Think about the Shortcuts you value and rely on to make your own life work. Now, twist that around and think about what would happen if you became a Shortcut who provided as your Shortcuts provide to you. What if *you* were someone who embodied everything that the rescuer did to me? You can be; all it takes is active participation and some elbow grease. It's something that changes your fortune in the workplace.

I'm guessing that you already have some degree of professional success and that you either want to maintain or enhance it. I'm also assuming the following scenario runs across your mind sometimes: you want to be more successful at work. You watch as others are. They seem to "have it all together," and you want some of that. It seems like you have all the goods to be the pick of the litter. But this success thing seems to remain on the tip of your tongue, and you just don't have everything you want.

You might even fall prey to the societal myths that dictate particular educational and career routes that lead you with certainty to the "throne of victory." So you might worry a bit and say to yourself that you didn't take that educational path, or that your career doesn't fit into a business magazine article's description of the ultra-accomplished. You might be hanging out in the middle of the career pack or trying for a more senior job, but somehow the next rung on the ladder remains elusive. You want to know what to do to get yourself the attention and the influence that will allow you to take better control of your future.

The good news is, you can make these changes, and this book will show you how. In fact, you're probably already doing some of what you need to do in order to get you there. As you read this book, you'll recognize yourself many times. At other times, the directives will seem so simple that you'll chastise yourself for not having followed them earlier. I believe you're probably reading this book because you already have everything you need to thrive, but somehow, it's just not kicking into full gear for you. Take a deep breath. It's a matter of reframing your mind-set and redirecting some of your energies. It's about being and using Shortcuts, and it will change your life.

Let the journey begin.

Introduction

First Things First: How a Shortcut Learns

> It is the childlike mind that finds the kingdom.
> —CHARLES FILLMORE
> *theologian*

Maria's face was moist, her voice almost a whisper. She was in tears as she began to talk. Not sobbing, uncontrollable kind of tears, but rather, the kind that comes with awe. For 19 years, Maria had been explaining to tourists what they were about to see on the famous ceiling of the Sistine Chapel—Michelangelo's masterpiece. Often, she would give a lecture before crossing into the chapel with a group of tourists so that when they entered it, among the throngs of others, they would be able to identify a few things in the three minutes they were given before being shoved out the other side. Up to 10,000 visitors proceed through the Sistine Chapel every day, and most get to brag just that they glimpsed it. Few ever are permitted to spend adequate time with it, to really *see* it in all its glory.

On the day our group met Maria, the Sistine Chapel had just begun allowing private tours after closing hours, for a very hefty sum. The company I was with had opted to pay the fee for its 250 employees who were on this incentive trip. Maria said jokingly that someone in our group must know the mafia to have secured such a perk. In her two decades as a guide, she had not been afforded the kind of time we would have in the Sistine Chapel, to beguile guests with her encyclopedic knowledge of the masterpiece.

So there we were, lying on the floor staring at the awesome grandeur of Michelangelo's work. We listened in silence for about 45 minutes as Maria took us through the masterpiece, her voice full of joy and wonder. It was one of the single most precious privileges I've had in my life. I don't mean the Sistine Chapel itself. Yes, it is stunning, and a must-see before exiting the planet; but I'm referring to the honor of being in the presence of a master historian like Maria. She helped us to *feel* as if we were in the Sistine Chapel on the day in 1512 when Michelangelo put on the last brushstroke of the work that many believe defines his life. We were as much in awe as she was.

When we were finished and back on the bus, I sat next to Maria and asked her what had been going through her mind when she was in the chapel. In her beautiful Italian-accented English she explained, "For me, the Sistine Chapel represents so much about what Italy brings to the world, and the history of all that is good and wonderful. I have not spent that much time uninterrupted in the Sistine Chapel since I began my tour work 19 years ago. When we were in the chapel and I was able to look upon the work slowly and deliberately—and lying on the ground, much as Michelangelo painted the ceiling—I saw it for the first time. I saw it how I hope you saw it—as a child. And so, it made me cry."

So it goes with anything in learning. You may have been exposed to the ideas I'm about to share; some of it through common sense, some of it as a "drive-by" learner. My hope is that as you read this, you will have an experience—like a child filled with wonder, awe, and questions—questions that make you stop fidgeting because you're thinking so hard. Lie down on the floor or in a favorite chair, look up and around, spend a few moments longer than usual reflecting on what this means to your life; and see yourself again for the first, spine-tingling, goosebump-making time.

Shortcut Quiz

My roommate says, "I'm going to take a shower and shave; does anyone need to use the bathroom?" It's like some weird quiz, where he reveals the answer first.

—MITCH HEDBERG
American comedian, 1968–2005

Everybody loves a good assessment, especially one that helps them develop into a stronger, more highly functioning individual. The Shortcut Quotient Inventory, or SQI, will help you learn about being and becoming a Shortcut. It is designed to provide you a place to start improving, and to heighten your awareness about ways to change your behavior. As you take it, answer honestly how *you are today,* not how you wish to be. Keep in mind, you can "cheat" just about any assessment, but it makes no sense to do that. It is only by being honest with yourself that you'll get a true idea of your areas of strength, as well as those of growth opportunity.

For the best results, take the SQI before reading ahead in the book, to get a clear view of yourself and so that you're not tempted to test for the "right" answers. With your answers in hand, you'll be able to read the rest of the book with greater purpose. Soon you'll be well on your way to becoming a highly influential Shortcut.

When you're ready, go to the Appendix to find the answers, with explanations.

Note

You can also take the quiz online, at www.BeAShortcut.com. You'll see how you measure up in all areas of being a great Shortcut. To gain access to the SQI®, enter code SQIBV when prompted. Enjoy!

The Shortcut Quotient Inventory (SQI)

1. Your company wants you to improve skills that are very specific to the organization. Your boss says that, unfortunately, he doesn't have money budgeted to pay for classes until next year. You:
   a. Find a class that you can afford, then let your boss know you've made arrangements for the class and tell him that any future reimbursement would be greatly appreciated.
   b. Let your boss know you'll check in periodically to see if the funds have been cleared for the class.

2. At the end of a very busy day at your current job, you most often:
   a. Feel tired and dissatisfied.
   b. Feel tired and satisfied.

3. There is an area of your job *right now* for which people would agree you are the best go-to resource in the company.
   a. True
   b. False

4. Your current job:
   a. Is constantly challenging to you and offers great opportunities to grow.
   b. Is something you can do without thinking about it.

5. If you could pick any career, you would:
   a. Explore something entirely different.
   b. Choose the one you're in.

6. Each year you purposefully take classes or find other educational opportunities to expand your professional knowledge and expertise.
   a. True
   b. False

7. When you feel overwhelmed and anxious in your job, you tend to:
   a. Get focused and get the work done the best you can.
   b. Find others to help you.

8. You often feel elation when you're doing the most difficult aspects of your job.
   a. True
   b. False

9. When you're angry with someone at work, you are most likely to:
   a. Have a discussion with him/her about what has made you angry.
   b. Let things be until they blow over.

10. Your boss obviously doesn't appreciate how busy you are and keeps piling on more work for you to do. You:
    a. Let her know you can take care of the requests, and with a smile let her know, gently, she owes you one.
    b. Sit down with her and have a discussion about workload.

11. You're on a deadline and you're behind. It's late in the day when a colleague comes by and asks for some help with her own impending deadline. She always acts as if her work is more important than yours. You:
    a. Inform her that now is a bad time for you because you're under your own deadline pressures. The last time you asked her for help, she told you the same thing.
    b. Explain that your deadline is looming and give her a time when you can help her. You also offer the names of others who can help if she needs immediate attention.

12. It feels to you as if your opinion is consistently disregarded by your supervisor. You:
    a. Express that you feel your opinions are not heard and that you would appreciate not being dismissed so readily.
    b. Express your opinion only when asked, even if you know that what you have to say would make your unappreciative boss look good.

13. When you are at work and it is very chaotic, you:
    a. Are very aware of the time passing.
    b. Lose track of the time.

14. Choose the statement that most accurately reflects your behavior when everyone seems to pile on the work for you:
    a. You set up proper expectations and let them know you have other work ahead of their request, unless it's an emergency that requires you to reprioritize your work.
    b. You inform the person requesting the task about when he/she can expect to have the job done.

15. You reach out weekly to people in both your personal and professional network just to check in.
    a. True
    b. False

16. You believe that those who get ahead professionally:
    a. Are competitive with others.
    b. Are collaborative with others.

17. When morale is bad at work. you can usually:
    a. Identify management decisions that are the reason.
    b. Identify your role in the bad morale.

18. When you choose a job, you:
    a. Look for a job that emphasizes personal life, but pays less.
    b. Look for a job that pays more but requires some personal sacrifice.

19. You are overwhelmed and busy. Your boss consistently asks you to take on additional work that is not a part of your job description. You:

a. Explain that you are happy to do it and detail how you propose to reprioritize this request with other tasks your boss has assigned.

b. Find a colleague or additional resources to help accomplish the task.

20. Your boss asks you to prepare a report to support his presentation to the executive committee. You:

a. Give him the report a little before it's due, and add a few things you think will be helpful in his presentation.

b. Give him the report far in advance of the due date so he'll have time to work with it.

21. Please indicate which statement is most accurate about you now:

a. I will do the work I am in now for the rest of my work life.

b. I think I will probably try other careers.

22. A client is angry about work you and others have done for her. You:

a. Listen carefully and then explain your role and the roles of each of the others so she will know who to talk to when addressing what went wrong.

b. Listen carefully; agree to communicate the issues to your colleagues; let the client know you'll get back to her with a solution.

23. An external caller mistakenly calls you with a question that belongs to a department with which you have no experience and no contacts. You:

a. Listen to the caller's question and ask him to hold while you find the right person to talk to. You determine the right person to direct the caller to, transfer the call, make an introduction, provide a brief explanation in a three-way connection, and then excuse yourself.

b. Save the caller time by stopping his request because you know the question is not for you. You direct him back to the main switchboard so he can be properly connected. You provide the main number for him to call.

24. An internal client has an expectation that you'll regularly do tasks that in the past you've done as a favor for her. These tasks are not part of your job description. The next time she asks, you:

    a. Politely remind her that in the past you've done this work as a favor and will do it one more time. After this you will need to make your own work a priority.

    b. Do the task as well as you can, then clarify with her afterward about her future expectations about these tasks.

25. It's Friday night. You're walking out the door of your office to go home for the evening, after a hectic and exhausting week. A coworker with whom you have no business and don't know well is busy assembling packets in the conference room. Your most likely reaction would be to:

    a. Offer to help as you're making your way to the door, knowing that he will likely tell you to go home.

    b. Tell him you have 30 minutes to give him a hand but have to leave after that.

26. When it comes to getting your job done, which is the most accurate statement about you:

    a. You're better at your job than most people to whom you would delegate the work, so it's better for you to do it.

    b. You find different people who can get the job done.

27. Think of your personal life: Which statement most accurately describes your weekends?

    a. I have plenty of time for myself.

    b. The majority of my time is spent running errands.

BE A
SHORTCUT

PART ONE

The Know-Why

Why to Be a Shortcut—From What It Takes to Why It's Worth It

> If we want to deserve more, we have to provide more.
> —NIDO QUBEIN
> *author, speaker, and president, High Point University*

THE SHORTCUT WAY

A Shortcut (according to the trusty dictionary) is:

- A shorter way to get to the same place.

- Any way of saving time, effort, expense, and so on.

When you think of MD, what comes to mind? How about PhD? *Consumer Reports? Harvard Business Review?* The FDA? These initials and titles usually conjure up a certain degree of respectability and know-how. The response is almost automatic. They are Shortcuts to the kind of information or service we're looking for from them. We don't have to question whether the information or service is reliable, because 9 out of 10 times it is. These people, groups, and publications stake their reputations on it. They've worked long and hard to get to that point. It's kind of like the parable of the old artist who was finishing up a painting in his studio as art students were being given a tour. The students came upon the artist and one of them remarked, "That's one of the most magnificent paintings I've ever seen! How long did it take you to paint it?"

The old artist replied, "Well, son, it took me two hours to put on the paint and 40 years to learn how."

Shortcuts take the time to be experts so that we don't have to. As a result, we're willing to pay for their artistry, their mastery, and know-how. They make it look easy. They make us feel as if we're doing them a favor for noticing their skills and using them. The relationship between the user of a Shortcut and the Shortcut is magical—and you can create that magic in your life both by being a Shortcut and availing yourself of the Shortcuts you select to go on your journey with you.

There are other kinds of Shortcuts that help us to get what we want. Think of a dazzling three-carat diamond ring, a yacht, a Mercedes-Benz, a fancy purse, or an expensive suit. Why do people buy these things at considerable expense when there are perfectly acceptable—and more affordable—alternatives? It boils down to a Shortcut, as well. These trimmings are Shortcuts to prestige, or at least the image of it.

When you're in a hurry, you look for a Shortcut to get you where you need to be. If you're in a hurry and you don't have much information, you *really* rely on a Shortcut. Here's an example: Consider when you're buying that last-minute birthday or holiday gift. You don't have a lot of time and you go to the mall just before the party is to take place. If you are like most people in this situation, you will overspend. Why? Because you use a highly ingrained Shortcut concept: expensive equals quality. That notion, coupled with lack of time and knowledge of the product, influences you to make the purchase. It's a reliable Shortcut, albeit sometimes costly. There are Shortcuts as equally entrenched in our brains as this one. Think about its opposite, for starters. Inexpensive equals cheaply made. Think of more. Home-cooked equals tasty. Organic equals healthy.

Human Shortcuts pop up in your life throughout your day. You use them to mow your lawn, cut your hair, clean your house, do your taxes, make stock picks for you, prepare your cup of joe, fix your lunch, wrap your gifts, paint your nails, give you a physical, wash your car—you get the picture. All of these examples have people attached to them who perform the Shortcuts for you. You are willing to pay money for the Shortcuts they provide, and your set of Shortcuts will be very different from someone else's, according to what you value.

Consider the following: You may use a lawn service to mow and fertilize your lawn and kill the weeds. However, you love to garden, so you dig holes, plant, mulch, trim, prune, and do anything else that's needed in the garden. Friends might wonder why, if you have a full lawn service, you don't have it do the gardening as well. It's simple: You value playing in the garden, but not hacking at grass or weeds. So, you pay for one service, but you would never pay for the other. Your friends who have no desire at all to dig around in the garden will pay someone to do that for them, or let it all go to seed or put in a no-maintenance rock garden. These same friends, however, will do their own income tax returns; they would never dream of paying someone to prepare them. You, on the other hand, loathe that activity and so you pay a Shortcut—your CPA— good money to do your taxes for you.

Now consider the ultimate business Shortcut, one that is not affected by the economy: the ATM. Hundreds of millions of people use automatic teller machines every day across the world, and pay the service fee when required, just for the convenience of getting cash more readily. The former Shortcut, writing a check, has essentially been replaced by the new Shortcut, composed of ATM machines and debit cards.

The trick in becoming a Shortcut is to frame yourself in the same indispensable way as the ATM. All commerce in the world exists because it provides a Shortcut to something or for someone. If you figure out what people want and need to have made more efficient in their lives, and you can provide it, you can nearly always get them to pay you for doing so. If they don't, then it's not a valued Shortcut. Don't waste your time on it. This, of course begs the question: Why would you want to be someone's Shortcut in the first place? Why would you want to do the bidding of others? After all, if they can do it, why shouldn't they do it themselves—you're busy doing your own thing! The answer is relatively simple.

People will judge your abilities based primarily on what you can do for them; but a close second is how you make them feel when you demonstrate your abilities. If you excel in an array of skills that are needed by other people who generally do not want to or cannot complete the tasks/skills themselves, you become valuable. If, then, you complete these tasks with a high degree of excellence, you become highly paid. And if you do these tasks for a lot of people, you become influential. Finally, if you master those skills and perform them with grace and a high degree of professionalism, you become powerful beyond compare.

Here's an example: Jenny is an executive administrator for the chief financial officer at a *Fortune 500* company. Any time I work with the CFO, I work with Jenny first. The cadre of things she does for this executive is vast—everything from what you'd typically expect to helping out on the occasional forgotten gift to protecting the CFO from unwanted or inappropriate meetings. She is the guardian of some of the most proprietary information in the organization. Jenny is the ultimate gatekeeper; and, says the CFO, "She saves my life." Jenny is never rude, always professional, appropriately personal, and one of the greatest Shortcuts for the lucky executive with whom Jenny *chooses to work.* That's right: Jenny is in the driver's seat. Her skills are impeccable, her ability to think one step ahead is remarkable, and she does it all with a brilliant attitude. Jenny is greatly valued and sought after; she is highly paid by anyone's standards, influential in many daily decisions at the highest level of the organization, and she controls the calendar and access to one of the most important officers of the company. That's power. That's what you get when you become a Shortcut.

On this odyssey to understand, use, and become a better Shortcut, here are a few things I'd like you to think about as you read this first part on being and using Shortcuts:

- What Shortcuts do you use in everyday life? The answer to this question will give you a clue to the value proposition of the Shortcut.

- Which Shortcuts do you use to make your life better at work?

- In what area in your life would you raise your hand to indicate you're the go-to person?

- Are you the kind of person about whom people feel good when they ask you to do something for them?

- Are you as influential as you would like to be? If not, think about where you would like more influence.

The next thing I'd like you to think about is the Shortcut formula. As you read, consider how you use and provide Shortcuts based on this formula. When an individual does not have one, two, or all three of the following elements for a certain task or job, they will be more likely to use a Shortcut:

- Time

- Talent

- Desire

If you or your company offers a Shortcut, ask yourself if any combination of the time, talent, or desire formula is being filled for a customer or colleague. For example, I always lease my car. Before I returned my last leased car, it was a mess of dog hair, tiny exterior scratches, and those scuffed-up black marks that mysteriously always appear on seats and the inside of the doors. I was running out of time to get the car cleaned and ready to return to the dealer in good shape, and I was lamenting that fact when a friend of mine told me about a guy who would come to my house, detail my car there, while I was working from home, and leave it in better shape than those quickie-detail places that really aren't so quick at all. I called the guy to make an appointment almost before the recommendation was out of my friend's mouth. I had no time, certainly no inclination, and most definitely no talent in the car detailing arena, so I paid the guy a premium to come out that afternoon. It was the best I've felt about spending money on something

I certainly could have done myself. He was, in short, the perfect Shortcut.

By the same token, my clients use me as a Shortcut to obtain the latest information and application of successful behavioral theory. Certainly, they could read through all of the research, and apply some of their own experiences to this field, but typically they don't have the time, inclination, or experience (talent) base to do it quickly and effectively. The formula works.

The following pages contain truths about Shortcuts. All of them point one way or another to the simple yet complex task of both using and being a Shortcut. The ideas are designed to provoke thinking about the Shortcuts you're willing to use and pay for, how you are a Shortcut, and how you can get more money and satisfaction for being a really good Shortcut yourself.

You are probably reading this because you want to be more effective at work; and, in general, Shortcuts are a remarkably useful tool in our personal lives as well. As you work through the chapters to come, apply the ideas about Shortcuts to your own situation. There may be times when you feel a little pang of guilt or discomfort because you're reading words about how *not* to be, and you see yourself in those words. Relax. I have yet to meet a human being who is "finished," while they are still alive. As Ian Percy, my good friend and philosophical speaker, says, "We're all unfinished human beings just making a go at this thing we call life."

Ponder the chapters; try to see yourself more clearly as you read them. Ask how you can be more of some things and less of others. It's all trial and error, and few ideas in the world should be swallowed whole, anyway. It takes practice to be a Shortcut; but in the long run, your life will be enriched both financially and emotionally. You'll more often feel that same delight as when you've done a favor for someone and he or she stands in awe of you, feels deep gratitude for what you've done, and is a little indebted to you. Not bad for just a little bit of Shortcut reading!

Back-Road Basics

The foolish seek happiness in the distance; the wise grow it under their feet.

—JAMES OPPENHEIM
American poet

Sometimes, people feel as if they're being naughty when they use a Shortcut. Some of the food for the best dinner parties I've hosted came straight out of plastic containers from Whole Foods—although I can take credit for spending the time to make the selections from behind the deli counter! Of course, I later emptied the delectable contents into my own serving dishes and tossed the evidence of its source into the trash outside. I used to feel guilty when I did this—because I *can* cook—until at one such party, I confessed when everyone began cooing about how great the food was. Afterward, one of the gourmet cooks in the group admitted she does the same thing more times than not, then adds a touch of this and that to the store-bought dishes, to make them "her own." Since that incident, I have lost all humility about using this Shortcut.

As with most Shortcuts, it doesn't make any sense to take the long road unless the Shortcut is unethical, illegal, or leads to shoddy work. The kind of Shortcut with a capital "S" is what we're talking about here; and not only is it a good thing, it's the way to thrive and survive in this incredibly busy and demanding world. Look around you and you will see that the winners in financial, personal, and spiritual endeavors—to name a few—all use excellent Shortcuts. They use Shortcuts so they can become Shortcuts themselves. Everyone intuitively wants in on the Shortcut action because we all know in our gut that that's how the world works.

Physical Shortcuts, or landmarks as most of us know them, are a powerful way to think of "people" Shortcuts. I've lived in Denver nearly all of my life. There's nothing like knowing a city inside and out, especially when severe weather is breaking loose and I'm stuck in rush-hour traffic. While all the out-of-state transplants are complaining about being trapped on a highway that looks like a parking lot, I can get from one end of the sprawling Denver metro area to the other by taking a series of back roads, and be home watching them on the news still stuck in the same place as when I took my detour. Mathematicians tell us that the shortest distance between two places is a straight line; it's also touted as the distance a crow flies. Well, I'm neither a mathematician nor a crow, and I'm more interested in time than distance. So, while I might travel 10 extra miles to get home on a route that isn't published in any GPS system, I'll get there more quickly because I know the Shortcuts. Shortcuts are for people who are interested in getting where they need to be in a more effective and efficient manner. It's not about doing so with bad quality, however. People often imply that taking a Shortcut means taking the easy, lesser-quality route. Yes, there are those kinds of shortcuts; but the purpose of this book is to focus on the kind that make us all do the "I could have had a V-8" slap on our foreheads because we didn't know about it sooner or think of it ourselves. You would be unlikely to hear a reasonable person who is stuck in traffic say, "No, I'm going to stay right here in this traffic for the next two hours to travel 10 miles because it's the main road, the quality road to take." They would take a Shortcut; and if one were miraculously delivered on that highway, I'd go out on an icy limb to say that they would gladly, gleefully, and joyfully give up some cash if that was required to get it. Shortcuts do that to a person; they feel like a rescuer to us—one worth paying for.

We are all so overwhelmed with the choices available to us today that we are actually becoming paralyzed in our ability to choose from among them. Shortcuts—the human variety—help others to wade through all of the options available, and they are paid handsomely for this service. They come in the form of real-tors, designers, building contractors, wedding consultants, meeting planners, executive coaches, lawyers, janitors . . . and the list goes on. We all want to make the best choice, and Shortcuts have taken the time to learn all about the choices so they can make recommendations to you based on your particular need.

Research psychologist Dr. Barry Schwarz is focused on the interesting topic of choice. His book, *The Paradox of Choice: Why Less is More*[1] delves deeply into why an abundance of choice is not necessarily good. He points out a very simple experiment per-formed in a grocery store: when there are several choices of fruit jam to sample, a person is a lot less likely to purchase a jar than when there are only a few to sample. That's right, fewer choices lead to a decision being made, whereas more choices cause peo-ple to often give up. It's paralysis by analysis. Schwarz also points out that an excess of choice often brings higher degrees of depres-sion and self-doubt. He asserts that the more apt we are to examine all of the choices available, the worse we actually feel. We might become paralyzed at the amount of choice offered to us. Whether we're contemplating a grocery store shelf or a major business deci-sion, we all need Shortcuts to help us wade through the variety of information and options now available to us.

Several years ago, personal shoppers came onto the scene. Yes, there are people who will do your grocery shopping for you. Personal shoppers will do everything from buying exactly the item and the brand on your list to getting general staples that you specify; but they make the choice about brand according to cost. That same kind of concierge service is cropping up in corporations everywhere. You can buy theater tickets, get your car serviced, order that birthday gift you forgot to buy, even get a massage.

Think of your own Shortcuts at work. If you've been around since the time when baby pictures were only in black and white, you might remember when sandwiches came out of a vending machine in little plastic, triangle-shaped packages. You did all of your errands before or after work, on weekends, and sometimes during your lunch break. When you went to the grocery store and you couldn't remember what your kids wanted, you had to wait to get to the store and find a pay phone to call home. If, when you called, you got a busy signal (this is the days before call-waiting), you had to call back later. Life was linear. It was one thing after the next, after the next, after the next. There was very little, if any, of this go to the dry cleaners, talk with a client on the phone on the way there while you're being e-mailed a contract, all the while scarfing down frozen yogurt or a quick burger kind of multitasking.

Shortcut Lesson

The irony of technology is that it has made things easier to accomplish at the same time it has made things more complex. We can now do more things more rapidly, but because more is now expected of us all the time, those technological wonders that make life easier actually make it more complex, as well. Thus, we now need to use Shortcuts because they are valuable to our well-being and success. Using products and services as Shortcuts is not a cop-out. We human Shortcuts are necessary, too, so that we can find sanity and time in life. The goal is to find an excellent set of Shortcuts. Great Shortcuts don't require you to give up quality, but they might require you to give up some money. The better and more necessary the Shortcut, the more cash you are usually willing to give. The same value and payment equation applies to you when you become a Shortcut. Round and round we go. Elton John and Tim Rice had it right. It's the "circle of life."

If You're Not a Shortcut You're Taking Up Too Much Space

Consider the postage stamp: its usefulness consists in the ability of sticking to one thing until it gets there.

—Josh Billings
nineteenth-century humorist

Can you think of a company that will keep someone on staff who is not a Shortcut to a business goal? When layoffs loom, business leaders must figure out who goes and who stays. It's a straightforward process with complex ramifications. The decision makers ask managers to provide a list of those who are providing "value-added" (read: good Shortcut) work.

Managers will then look around and ask themselves some simple questions:

- Who is "high maintenance?"

- Who gets things done without having to be told—or at the very least, not told twice?

- Who preempts my very thoughts and needs?

- If I did away with a certain position, would it negatively affect the organization?

- Do I have Shortcuts in my organization who are so good that they can pick up the relatively minor Shortcuts a person in question is providing?

If you're one of those people who has gotten laid off recently, you might feel a little offended right now. But, if you think about this from a business perspective, you'll be able to layoff-proof yourself more effectively in the future. If you're in "forced retirement" right now—or ever have been—think about what you do in your personal life. You downsize. You cut back. You start to look at where your money goes and make decisions about where you'll continue to spend and where you won't. You probably have a formal or informal process of elimination, and somehow you come up with a list of things that are indispensable to your survival during this downtime. When it gets really tough, you make decisions based on the things that bring the utmost value and positive impact to your current situation. You want the least amount of frustration during a frustrating time. That's what businesses do: they decide between the nice-to-have and the need-to-have. Become a need-to-have by becoming an excellent Shortcut.

One of the steps toward achieving that goal is to avoid being a high-maintenance employee. I'll discuss that in depth in Part Three, the know-how section of the book, but it bears mentioning at this early stage. A high-maintenance individual—no matter how smart and accomplished he or she is—eventually gets looked over, and could, therefore, get the axe.

One of my clients came to me after a workshop on attitude and its impact on the bottom line. She asked for some advice. "Scott," she began, "this guy who reports to me, and who I hired, is one of the most capable people I know. He's smart and experienced, but I'm not sure what to do with him because he's disrespectful and dismissive to people who are below his peer level. I'm cleaning up after him everywhere I go. I've had chats with him about how he handles people. He says he understands, but then a few weeks later he's back to his passive-aggressive, dismissive and condescending behavior. He just makes people feel not very smart when they're with him. I don't have time for this, and I'm afraid I'm going to lose a few people who work for him if something doesn't happen soon. What should I do?"

The short answer is easy on the surface, but we all know that it's more complex than just giving this employee a pink slip, especially if he's demonstrating excellent skill and you want to keep him. However, there is a point of diminishing return, and high-maintenance individuals—people who have to be looked after, swept up after, coddled, and have their egos massaged—hit a threshold point, at which time their experience and skills no longer matter as much as they once did. You see this phenomenon at all levels in every industry in the world.

My client's eyes lit up with complete understanding when I responded initially, "You have a high-level, high-maintenance worker, and you're wrestling with the dilemma, 'do I keep him or them?'" When you find yourself in the same predicament or, perhaps worse, recognize that this person is you, you're facing the taking-too-much-space truth, and something is about to happen.

My advice to this manager was: "Let him know you value his intelligence and experience, but those represent only half of what it takes to secure his future at the organization. The other half is his interaction with his subordinates. Tell him you'll judge him in the future on his ability to bring out the best in his support people."

My client and I continued the conversation about remedies, but she quickly and clearly saw that her employee was generating more work for her than he was worth to the organization. He was high maintenance, a prima donna whose performance was not worth the trail of wounded workers he left behind. He was no longer a Shortcut.

Other high-maintenance scenarios involve employees who need so much reinforcement or oversight that the person to whom they should be a Shortcut finds him- or herself spending too much time with that employee. It's understandable when someone is new on the job; but after about six months, often, a little bell goes off, signaling the recognition that the learning curve is flattening out, and it's time for this person to be doing a lot of this work on his or her own. I've lost count of the number of scenarios presented to me that involve the high-maintenance individual, and they're rarely about skill and aptitude.

In contrast, those smart, capable people who are low maintenance are the ones we all admire. They are Shortcuts to achieving the goals of the business, and they remove obstacles to getting things done. In my own business, I have the awesome luxury of being a small organization staffed entirely by Shortcuts. But not too long ago, I was being a bad leader. I was talking with one of our valued colleagues, Marci, during an overwhelming period, and I was getting the hint from her that I was failing to acknowledge the amount of work she was performing on a regular basis. This is not something she usually points out, but even the lowest-maintenance colleagues need some recognition of their worth. I know this, but I somehow lost sight of it. So, as Marci and I talked, she unwittingly helped me define low maintenance.

"Sometimes, Scott," she said, "I don't think you know all of the many details and moving parts we pull together to get you out the door and to an engagement." Marci and her colleagues do yeoman's work every day, and when I'm running at full speed, all I know is that I have the information I need to be where I need to be to do what I need to do. No complaints from her or the others. It is the nature of this beast.

I replied, "You're right, Marci, and that is exactly why you are such an incredible Shortcut to me. I don't have to think about or hear about all of the details. I just know they'll be taken care of, and clients gloat about you, unsolicited." Marci was describing the low-maintenance Shortcut. She hollers if she needs something; but for the most part, she figures it out by herself—and I have no detailed idea of the fires and near-misses and client frustrations that go on behind the scenes. If I need to know, she brings me up to speed and then I get involved; otherwise, I do my thing because she does her thing, so well.

Thanks, Marci (I feel like I just did a "Hi Mom" on network TV).

Shortcut Lesson

You can see it as a bumper sticker: If you're not a Shortcut to someone, you're taking up too much space (and will probably be replaced with someone who is a Shortcut). The higher maintenance you become—and the more you develop a bad attitude, need for attention, or anything else that causes people to have to work around you—the less space on the ledge you have. If you scored low in the emotional intelligence part of the Shortcut Quiz, you might be high maintenance. Pay attention, and learn from the know-how section of the book.

Are You a Shortcut or Bottleneck?

> If you give one person the ability to be the bottleneck,
> you'll have to kiss his butt if you want anything done.
> —WARREN WILSON
> *journalist*

When the Denver International Airport (DIA) first opened in October 1995, it was the most modern airport in the world. Its avionics were hailed as state of the art; it was one of few airports in the world that could simultaneously land three jumbo jets side by side; its concourse boasted a layout excellent for travelers; and it was visually stunning, if not at least an architectural oddity. All of this was lost on the flying public because of a major bottleneck that plagued the airport's opening: the baggage system. This one failing undermined so much of what was brilliant about DIA that to this day the airport suffers from bad-mouthing of its baggage system; although the major kinks have been ironed out and it is currently not any worse than those at other major airports. After more than a dozen years, the facility is still backpedaling. All I have to do is tell someone in another airport that I'm from Denver and, invariably, he or she will ask, "Did they get the baggage system fixed yet?"

DIA never opened its planned multimillion-dollar, futuristic baggage system on schedule because it mangled bags so badly during test runs they were rendered unrecognizable. Just as bad was that luggage often was misdirected—some bags ended up in Bermuda when they should have gone to Boise. In short, the problems with the system prevented the world's newest aviation wonder to open. In fact, replacing the ill-fated system with the old reliable one was one of the chief causes for the year-and-a-half delay, and caused the project to run $2 billion over budget. And because DIA had touted the baggage system loudly and often, travelers sat up and took notice. The newfangled system, said DIA, would make luggage transfer from one flight to the next efficient and accurate, allowing connecting passengers to be worry-free. For travelers whose final destination was DIA, the new system meant no more lost bags.

DIA took a gamble on an important Shortcut for travelers, but then took a hit because it didn't deliver. People don't want their Shortcuts messed with. Once they have a good Shortcut, they expect it to be reliable—no exceptions.

Shortcut Lesson

The lessons from this botched-up Shortcut-turned-bottleneck are many. First, be careful if you brag about your Shortcut abilities. Make sure it works before you trumpet the Shortcut to others. Second, the DIA story is another excellent example of how easily you can tarnish the image you worked so hard to earn and, conversely, how difficult it is to restore a good reputation. And, finally, there's a lesson here on human nature. Once you've promised or unleashed your service or product as a Shortcut, people will hold you to the high standard you espouse and punish you if you don't deliver. Privilege and responsibility are difficult to separate when it comes to being a Shortcut.

Determining Your Value

Economics is the method; the object is to change
the soul.

—Margaret Thatcher
former British prime minister

When I was in high school, my mom gave me a poster with the words, "I want what I want when I want it" to describe the behavior I had often displayed. This statement summarizes how people feel about the Shortcuts they want in their lives. If you say they can have the Shortcut, they want it *now*. There are no take-backs. If you do have to take something back, punishment is meted out through low trust. Just look at software delays, new hardware developments, or store openings. If they run late, there is a price to pay in customer enthusiasm and loyalty.

When you look at the Shortcut you're promising, be careful. People will cling more to the Shortcuts they deem essential such as, "getting my luggage *immediately* when I get to baggage claim." However, people will make the Shortcut pay dearly if the promise isn't delivered. You have to spend a lot of time and/or money to overcome the bad PR.

The chart shown on page 19 is designed to give you some idea of how valuable you are as a Shortcut. For it to be accurate, rate yourself, and then ask others who know your work or product to make a rating.

First, however, remember that the formula for a good Shortcut is when a potential consumer of your product or service lacks time, talent, or desire in regard to your offering. If he or she has a need for one of these things, and you can fulfill the need, you're a good Shortcut. If the person lacks two, and you can fulfill both, you're a *very* good Shortcut; and if the person lacks all three and you can fulfill them all, then you're an excellent Shortcut. But that's only a part of the equation. If you apply good old Economics 101 to it, you'll be able to determine your value as a Shortcut and adjust accordingly. Look at the chart: it's made up of cost and need. Basically, the lower the cost for someone to use your service, the better off you are as a Shortcut. The level of need for your service determines its value. If you have the magical mix of low cost/high need, then you are a Shortcut who will have extraordinarily high value.

THE FIVE-STAR SHORTCUT: THE HIGHEST-VALUE MARK

A *high value mark* is the highest score a Shortcut can have, so you're a five star if you have the highest value (like a five-star rating for a hotel). This rating says that you or your product will most likely be blessed with the elixir of success and influence: high volume and high value. If you're an individual Shortcut, this means that more people will come to know you as a resource, and will pay you top dollar for that five-star ranking.

An example of a five-star service is H&R Block for tax preparation, or Grease Monkey and Jiffy Lube for an oil change. I absolutely need these services, and the cost is relatively low; so I don't

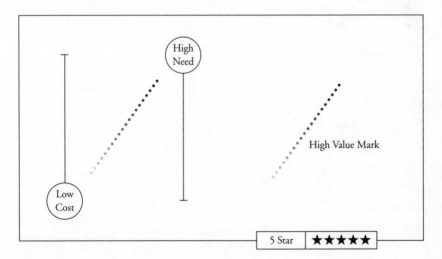

think a lot about using the services, I just do. If you're an individual or service organization with a five-star rating, you probably have highly specialized knowledge or abilities; or you fall into that category of doing something that must be done that no one really wants to do themselves. Some physicians, house cleaners, lawn services, administrative support, executives with a specialized skill, and computer "geek squads" are examples of people who have the highest possible value at low cost; therefore, they are all great Shortcuts.

THE THREE-STAR SHORTCUT: THE NEUTRAL ZONE

If you're a three-star Shortcut—low need/low cost—you're in the neutral zone, and you might see high volume, but more value judgments will be made about your service or product. For instance, valet parking is a great Shortcut, especially at the mall during the holiday season. Do I *need* the service? Probably not; but at the right price, I'll likely use the service, especially if I'm in a hurry. If it's a nice day in the middle of the summer, however, I will value that

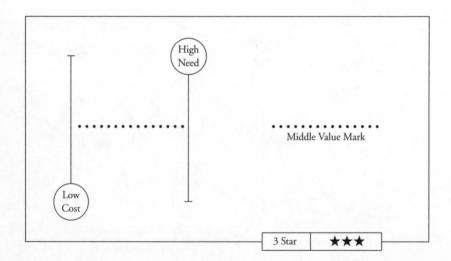

same Shortcut less, so the cost would need to go down even further to get me to use it, if I use it at all.

The other neutral mark at three stars is high need and high cost. It is a fine Shortcut box to be in, but again, judgments will be made—in this case with regard to cost. Volumes are usually lower in this quadrant, but fees and prices go up because fewer people are highly trained in the high need area. Specialty physicians fit into this category, as do certain attorneys, CEOs, CFOs, some accountants, luxury automobiles, house painters, and renovation contractors. But you and your product are in danger of moving into the no-star category if your cost goes so high that you or your products are deemed to be "nothing I need." Let's take a look at this scenario—because this is where the Shortcut can lose its luster.

THE NO-STAR SHORTCUT: LOWEST-VALUE MARK

If you or your product fit into the criteria for the no-star mark—low need and high cost—it's time to rethink what you're offering. This scary ranking means that you're probably going to go out of business

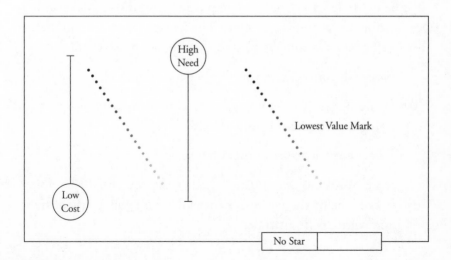

or lose your job. It means that the price you want me to pay for the product or service you render is more than I am willing to pay. Let's say you start out as a high need for me: administrative assistance. You require a fair market value for payment. Eventually, you take on an "attitude"—a bad one. The job is no longer fresh to you and you make it known, loud and clear. You start pushing back on many of the requests that I make; in this way, it becomes more about your comfort and your needs than mine. Your "cost" goes up because I'm spending more time dealing with your bad attitude, figuring out ways to work around you, and so on. The cost in terms of time and money goes way up. I have to spend more time thinking about how to approach you so that I don't set you off. I take on some of the tasks I formerly assigned to you so I won't have to deal with your bad attitude and pushback. Or I have to redo or have someone else do certain tasks. The cost is high. Clearly now, my need for you has diminished. As your cost goes up and your value goes down, you are in danger of becoming obsolete.

This applies to that high-maintenance person I described earlier. Think about someone who is supposed to be a Shortcut for you, such as the administrative assistant in this example. You end up not giving the administrator, house cleaner, clerk, or research person certain pieces of work that he or she should be doing because it is being done wrong, is not completed on time, or comes with a lot of snide looks and heavy sighs. This person's days are numbered because he or she is moving toward the dreaded no-star rank.

- Now, ask yourself, are you this person?

- Is the person for whom you are supposed to be a Shortcut doing dances around your moods?

- Does your client/boss/other often have to redo your work?

- Is he or she holding on to certain tasks you should be doing because he or she no longer trusts that you will do them right and without the attitude?

If you answered yes to one or more of these, it's time to evaluate what you think you're being paid to do in the first place. By the same token, you can ask these questions about the Shortcuts who work with or for you. The answers might shed light onto that age-old question of what's going on with that person who used to be so "into" the job.

You can rank yourself or your product as a Shortcut. The lower the cost and the higher the need to others, the more frequently a Shortcut will be used. That demand leads to a good deal of influence in pricing and negotiations. Cost is measured in both time and money. If it costs me a lot of time to work with you because of your attitude or lack of skill, your value goes down, and so does your influence.

Rehab Tactics for the Chronic No-Star

Many people want to know how to "rehab" a once-excellent Shortcut. This sidebar is aimed at giving you some ideas to help out. It's also for those of you who recognize yourselves as no-star Shortcuts (which, by the way, is an excellent first step to your own rehab). The lessons described here will guide you through the hard work of changing your own behavior. Better yet, share these lessons with someone who is willing to help you along the journey. It will shorten the time it takes to get on the right track and become a five-star Shortcut.

Read the following in context to your needs: Are you helping a former Shortcut, or are you a has-been Shortcut yourself?

If your Shortcut is not behaving like a Shortcut any longer, this is a good time to have a conversation with him or her. Something is about to give anyway. The former Shortcut will either storm off the job, burning bridges as he or she goes, or you will have to give the person the pink slip. All the data show that it is far less expensive to rehabilitate a knowledgeable worker than to hire and train a new one. Of course, that has its point of diminishing returns. But if you haven't yet had the heart-to-heart chat about performance, start by:

- Making a list of the things you hired this person to do in the first place. Or, if you "inherited" the employee with your job, write down the things you admire about his or her abilities.

- Making a list of the attributes and attitudes that seem to be getting in the way of that work.

- Keeping these items in the back of your mind as you interview the person, in your quest to find out what's going on.

- Asking questions such as: "Jill, I can't help but notice lately that you seem to be distracted and aren't working the way you used to. Is there something upsetting you, or is something wrong?"

- Preparing examples of what you are disturbed about. Be specific. If Jill asks for examples, your completed lists will help you specify something such as: "Jill, you used to seem so happy about your job and being here. Now, it seems as if you're angry about something most of the time. More specifically, and in terms of how it impacts your performance, you used to write such complete reports for my poststaff meetings. Now, they're bare bones, and I have to push you to get them to me in a timely manner, and even then you do so with a sour attitude."

- Being prepared to learn something that requires or allows you to help salvage this person who was once a valued Shortcut.

You will know what to do as the interview progresses. The intention is to find out why the once-great Shortcut has become a bottleneck. Your goal is to get the person back on track. If you are going to fire the individual and haven't had this conversation yet, I would strongly recommend that you have one like it the next time you're in this situation. Not only is it the decent thing to do with problem employees, it's a relatively expedient and safe way to get at what might be happening in the background for a Shortcut. Sometimes, delicate topics are difficult to articulate and many people have no idea how to broach them.

Here's an example: Sandy, an executive with whom I worked in emotional intelligence, discovered that she was low in empathy, which really came as no surprise to her (and she didn't care!). The bombshell went off when she was able to think back to a recent situation at the office when her administrator—a normally excellent worker—began to show up with a bad attitude and seemed angry upon receiving simple job instructions. Initially, Sandy ignored the behaviors, as someone with low empathy will tend to do, instead focusing on the results. Her Shortcut had become a no-star, and Sandy was perplexed. After she acknowledged her low empathy, and came to understand how it could affect those around her, Sandy had an epiphany. She asked her administrator to go to lunch with her. She described it as a "just catching up" lunch. During the meal, she asked a lot of questions, and really listened to the answers. Through the discussion, she uncovered that her administrator was being abused at home and was filing for a divorce. Sandy had been too busy and lacking in the skills to notice when her administrator gave subtle signs that something was wrong. The spiral downward began and the five-star Shortcut became a no-star in a hurry.

The lesson here? You can often find out how a Shortcut is diminishing in value if you start by asking what's going on. Most people don't go from exemplary Shortcut to pain-in-the-backside seemingly overnight without a compelling reason. Ask.

The point is that you must acknowledge the background noise one way or another, because you are probably not the only one noticing it. Besides, if you were a five-star Shortcut and something in your life plummeted you into no-star status, wouldn't you want to be given a second chance?

If you are indeed the one who has gone from five-star to no-star status and recognize yourself here, it will require courage to take the initiative and talk with your boss about what is happening in your world. Hopefully, your situation will not be as serious as that which affected Sandy's administrator, but if you have become a costly person to keep around, it must be dealt with. There is no guarantee that your boss will jump up and down for joy because you recognize that you have become a pain in the backside, but it is a start to seeing stars in your future.

Shortcut Lesson

The very best Shortcuts, whether individuals or products, are five-stars on the Shortcut Value Chart. There is a high need and a relatively low price for what they have to offer. People go to them or buy the product at elevated volumes. The three-star Shortcuts are in the neutral zone and have to be more vigilant, monitoring both cost and value because if their value slips lower than what people are willing to pay, stars are lost. The non-Shortcut group—the no-star zone—is the place where you must start asking questions of the person (including yourself) or product that has dipped into that place. Once in the no-star zone, if the person or product cannot be changed, they will probably become obsolete very quickly.

Anatomy of a Bottleneck

> Outside of traffic, there is nothing that has held this
> country back as much as committees.
>
> WILL ROGERS
American humorist

Tom is a traffic engineer I met at a dinner party. If we had
stopped talking after I heard his scintillating title, I would have
missed a fascinating lesson about traffic and a major lesson about
life. I learned from Tom that a traffic engineer is, basically, an expert
on flow. I took the opportunity to ask for his insight about a particularly troublesome segment of I-25 in Denver that was being reen-
gineered because of its nightmarish traffic jams. The area is referred
to as "the Narrows of I-25." It is only about 4 miles long, but it
might as well have started in Montana with the major backups
it traditionally caused.

"Everyone I know avoids it," I said to Tom, "so I'm intrigued as
to why it slows to a crawl every rush hour," I asked Tom.

Tom explained, "A few small things can slow down and impede
traffic flow, even when there are no accidents on the highway. The
Narrows were built with a reduced shoulder space of about a foot
on each side of the highway, in order to fit between the neighbor-
hoods through which it cuts—thus the term, the Narrows. It also
had several badly spaced exit and entrance ramps, one after the
next. The last thing is that the highway was not straight. It curved
through the Narrows. All of these things added up to one of the
worst man-made traffic problems anywhere in the country."

When a multibillion-dollar reconstruction of I-25 was carried out in the years between 2000 and 2007, the Narrows was
one of the first items on the drawing board. It was widened and

straightened and the ramps were redesigned. The result is nothing short of a miracle. Traffic flows and capacity have significantly increased. The highway has gone back to being what it was intended to be in the first place: a rapid way to get from one point to another through the city.

Shortcut Lesson

When a Shortcut (in this case, highway I-25) creates or becomes a bottleneck, eventually people will take a different route and circumvent the bottleneck just to avoid the headache of dealing with it.

Most of us have experienced bottlenecks at work, those processes that put the wrench in the spokes and slow everything down. Bottlenecks can be people who, on first blush seemed to be Shortcuts but over time developed an "I don't have time" or "you do it if you want it done" attitude. They began to behave in ways that, ironically, made it easier for you to take the more difficult route.

Either the bottleneck has to be fixed or it will eventually be replaced. Be a Shortcut, not a bottleneck.

Shortcuts Save Time

> Time is more valuable than money. You can always get
> more money, but you can't get more time.
>
> —JIM ROHN
> *author and speaker*

I was spending a lot of time in New York City because of my job.
Lisa Searchinger, one of my coworkers, and a native of New
York, was showing me around. We were looking for a place to
eat when I spied a Thai restaurant. I love Thai food and made a
move to go in. But as I started to pull open the door, Lisa shrieked,
"Stop!" Startled and amused, I listened as she asked/demanded:
"Don't you know the cardinal rule of eating in the city?" I guessed
I didn't, judging from the purple shade her lips had turned over my
near-fatal mistake. She proceeded to tell me one *never* walks into
a restaurant in New York that has not been recommended if no
one else is eating there. I looked through the plate-glass window,
and sure enough, the place was empty. Clearly, the Shortcut formula to dining in Manhattan is, "no people equals don't eat there."
Conversely, if the place is overcrowded, with people spilling out
onto the sidewalk, it is acceptable to wait two hours to eat.

We take Shortcuts like Lisa's because of the deluge of information and choices at our disposal. We couldn't possibly know
all there is to know about most things. So we have to take our
cues from a variety of different sources. Shortcuts are time-savers.
If you had to get a recommendation on every restaurant in New
York before going into it, you'd never go out to eat. So the Big
Apple rule is one that natives seem to learn as if by osmosis. It
becomes ingrained, and it saves them time. There are a few others we have locked just below our consciousness. This time-saving

device is called "social proof." We've become accustomed to taking quick Shortcut cues from social situations when we are uncertain, such as in the Thai restaurant scenario. Neither Lisa nor I knew whether this was a good dining spot, but the quick Shortcut cue was, simply, to glance inside. Think about the last time you were in a Starbucks or other coffee shop where they put out tip jars. I have been the first person in a coffee shop in the morning and have witnessed a shop employee put out a tip jar with one of his own dollars in it. Social proof says, "If others are giving their extra money, then I should, too, even if it's only a little bit of change." It works for the most part. It is a Shortcut to making a decision.

Robert Cialdini, PhD is my guru on this topic. He has written a few books about influence[2, 3] and the things that compel us to comply. He tells of many an unconscious choice that is made because of influencers we use to help us make decisions amidst all the chaos. One of the strongest and least conscious is social proof. To see this in action, next time someone tells an off-color joke at a party, watch people's reactions. There will be a few who automatically start laughing nervously. Another group will stay on the fringe, looking around to see if anyone else thinks it's funny before they chime in with their own mercy laugh. You will see this behavior in corporations when the big wig has laid a joke bomb on an employee audience. There is usually a delay, while people try to inconspicuously catch a glimpse of others' faces—difficult to do when everyone is facing His or Her Highness. So, typically, the laughter begins slowly and politely ripples through the audience. The giggles only really start when a few brave souls decide to strike out on their own and give a big ha-ha. Then it's acceptable for others to follow.

Another form of social proof takes place when we look at advertising. Which shampoo or toothpaste do we buy? Advertisers will often take the "used by more [mothers, teens, men, doctors, and so on] than any other brand" route. That is social proof at its most apparent, and it's a Shortcut we all subconsciously use.

Again, it boils down to a time-saver we've somehow incorporated into ourselves. We all love a great time-saver, so that's what the best Shortcuts provide.

The use of authority is another influencer that leads to unconscious, time-saving Shortcut decisions. Many people will instantly fall into step when they see another person dressed in a certain uniform of authority. The famous Stanley Milgram[4] studies of 1974 illustrated this phenomenon in its full splendor.

> Two study volunteers are ushered into a room, where they are met by two white lab-coated experts. One of the volunteers is deemed the teacher, the other the learner. The learner is strapped into something akin to an electric chair. The teacher is taken by the experts into a room with a two-way mirrored window. The learner is told that he will be asked several questions in increasing difficulty. For each one he answers wrong he will receive an electrical zap. For each subsequent incorrect answer, the voltage zap will be successively higher. Though the zap is administered under the tutelage of the experts, the teacher is the one who pulls the trigger.
>
> At first, the learner gets several of the answers correct. After the first incorrect answer and subsequent zap, the wrong answers become more frequent, probably due to stress. The teacher meanwhile is turning up the dial on the zapping apparatus. The zaps become so intense that the learner begins to holler. He then begins kicking and screaming. He can't get out of the chair because he is strapped into it. The voltage meter reads a stunning amount of voltage. It is one heck of a zap.

There is more to the experiment, but you get the idea. What you might not know is that the guy in the electric chair is an actor, who pulls off the fried human scene very well. The teacher, however, really is an unknowing volunteer. The study showed that the teacher—even though visibly very distressed—kept administering the zaps because the guys in the lab coats told him to do so. When the teacher protested, he was told to go ahead and do it anyway. And he did! When the two white coats got into an argument over whether a very high voltage zap should be given, the teacher became frozen and shouted that the white coats should make up their minds. They did; he was told to give the zap, and the learner went berserk. Even though the teacher is practically whimpering, he is complying with the requests of the lab coats.

Milgram's study demonstrates that something as simple as a white lab coat gives a person unchallenged authority. We unconsciously use the white coat as a symbol of, in this case, scientific knowledge and experience and high standards. We say to ourselves that these professionals must know what they're doing, so we comply. Uniforms and logos are Shortcuts; and they are so powerful that they can lead us to make a decision we might not otherwise make.

We make unconscious time-saving choices based on titles, too, choices that are sometimes inaccurate. In medical offices across the country, there are those patients who refuse to see a physician's assistant (PA) or nurse practitioner (NP), even though both groups are highly trained medical professionals, many of whom have prescription privileges. Doctors will tell you that even in the most complex cases, PAs and NPs are excellent caregivers. They always work in conjunction with a physician and will not make decisions or diagnoses for which they are not trained. But their titles get in the way. People want to see an MD, a medical doctor, not someone with "assistant" or "nurse" attached to their title. "MD" implies that the person bearing the title has expended many years of blood, sweat, and toil, and so most people associate it with a high level of expertise. Shortcuts—such as the one we assign to the initials of MD—serve us well most of the time. But they also can be the opposite of a time-saver, in the long run. If you go into an emergency room and insist on seeing an MD instead of an NP or PA, unless you have a sucking chest wound, the NP or PA may be just what the doctor ordered to get you feeling better faster.

Lest you think you are not under the automatic pull of this kind of authority, check your pulse as you check your speedometer the next time you pass a police car.

Shortcut Lesson

Human beings are seemingly wired to look for and respond to Shortcuts. It's part of an evolutionary process to save us time so that we don't have to think of every step and every detail in a more chaotic environment. Most of the time, those Shortcuts serve us well—such as in the examples of social proof and authority. There are instances, however, when Shortcuts are not accurate, as described in the case of PAs and NPs. Nothing is 100 percent, not even a great Shortcut. One thing is certain, however: a good Shortcut gives you the greatest gift of all—time.

PART TWO

The Know-What

How to Be a Shortcut

> Clarity of mind means clarity of passion, too; this is why a great and clear mind loves ardently and sees distinctly what he loves.
>
> —BLAISE PASCAL
> *Seventeenth century French mathematician and physicist*

THE CASE IS CLEAR

It is obvious that we need Shortcuts to be excellent. Clearly, we all use Shortcuts unconsciously, and we love it when we find good ones. And it is apparent that to be an excellent Shortcut ourselves, we need excellent ones to support us. It is clear—the world is indeed circular and we are all connected through the service given us and that which we give to others. It makes the world go 'round. Be a Shortcut. It's good for your life.

Make It Easier, Make It Better, Make More Money

> Everybody is looking for the magic pill. But commitment is an ongoing process. It's not something you do once. You revisit it.
>
> —PATRICIA KYLE
> *university professor and psychologist*

No matter what field of work you toil in, chances are you have had to do some sort of presentation—some persuading, some convincing, or some informing, in order to get your business done. At times, your presentation may have been fancy, with PowerPoint bells and whistles to beat the band. Or maybe you've just had to deliver your product or service to a single customer. Perhaps it has just been you trying to make a case with your boss for doing something differently in your job, or angling for a promotion. Regardless of the situation, when it comes to making your proposal, your goal as a Shortcut should be to answer yes to all of the following three questions. Consider these as starting points as you prepare your presentation:

- Will what you're proposing make your listener's life or job *easier*?

- Will what you're proposing make your listener's life or job *better*?

- Will what you're proposing make your listener *more money*?

If you can answer yes to all three, you're likely to be a hit and will sell your audience. You will have that client, that sale, that promotion—whatever it may be—in the bag. If you can answer yes to just one, you'll have delivered some of the goods, and sometimes that will be enough; at the very least, you'll be traveling in a Shortcut direction. If you can't answer yes to any of these questions, reconsider what you're asking for, and, more important, how you're asking for it.

But take note: Effective Shortcuts don't wait for a presentation to offer suggestions to their colleagues and managers. They are constantly on the lookout for ways to make one of the big three—easier, better, more money—happen. If you employ these three questions (really, think of them as guidelines) on a regular basis when presenting at a meeting or in a one-on-one situation, your audience, whether one or many, probably marvels at your wisdom and the value you bring to the organization.

EASIER

Find a way to ease the day for people—even if it means removing just one to-do item from their list.

Consider Sandra, a model Shortcut at work. She makes sure that the people she reports to regard her as someone who can make their jobs easier. She doesn't brag about all of the things she does, but rather says things like, "That's something I can do for you. You can focus on something else." She almost insists upon taking care of things at which she deems herself to be an excellent Shortcut. Her can-do attitude is inspiring, and it's all about making the lives of others easier. Conversely, she expects the same approach from the people who support her.

What is Sandra's reward for being a Shortcut who uses the "easier" tactic? Society assigns a great deal of competence to people who have the ability to find the easier route. We all cheer them, especially when we're under pressure and can't find the easier way ourselves. Your value goes up as you are deemed more competent.

When you use this Shortcut tactic, you are, in essence, strutting your stuff—demonstrating how competent you are.

BETTER

Give someone a way to look good to the people who matter most to them. Suggest something that will increase their quality of life.

Sandra, our model Shortcut makes a proposal to her boss that seems costly, but has some benefits in the long term, by paying off in enormous revenue. She does her homework; preparing the proposal for her boss while keeping in mind he is interested in looking good to his manager. She learns that the hot buttons for her boss's manager involve growing revenue in innovative ways, so she focuses her proposal sharply on that goal.

Sandra provides a Shortcut to her boss to look good to his manager. She takes the time to do her homework. Her argument is incredibly persuasive. Her boss is going to look smart to his manager. It's a done-deal.

Again, what does Sandra get for making her boss look better? Doesn't she run the risk of never getting credit for her ideas? Yes, there are some people out there who will always claim another's ideas as their own. But, let's revisit the value proposition:

- First, Sandra has a history of developing ideas that make her supervisor and others look better, so she has become more valuable. When it comes time to negotiate a raise or a promotion, Sandra has built a good deal of trust and loyalty with her boss and colleagues for her input and ideas.

- Second, being an excellent Shortcut does not mean being a pushover. You can claim ideas as your own and ask others to expand upon them, help you with them, or take them as their own to help in their work. If you need to look good, then go get Shortcuts who will help you do that. If you want to be a Shortcut, helping others look good is part of the equation.

- Finally, consider the alternative. You hoard ideas that might make others look good so that, by default, they don't look that much better than you. That's a pretty Machiavellian approach to life and a miserable existence in anyone's book. Look around you. The people you are attracted to and who you want in your sphere are those who take the time to make you look good. Sometimes, you have to take the backseat so that you know how it feels when you're in the front seat.

MORE MONEY

Help someone make money or cut costs. Enough said.

If you have to default to only one of the three goals, the most persuasive and best Shortcut is going to be different for every person. If the person you're trying to convince is lured by material things, then use the money persuader. If he or she is impressed with titles and hobnobbing with important people, the "better" tactic will work well to persuade them. And, if the person appears harried and burnt out, you might try an argument that makes his or her job easier. If you don't know for certain, making someone money or making the person look impressive are pretty safe bets.

Shortcut Lesson

Make the three-part formula a mantra: Easier, better, more money. Easier, better, more money. Easier, better, more money . . .

The best Shortcuts strive to make this formula come alive in all aspects of their work for others. They are Shortcuts by making a Shortcut for others.

The Shortcut of Efficiency (Easier)

> Efficiency is doing better what is already being done.
> —PETER DRUCKER
> *management expert*

Six Sigma (the process perfection system), Total Quality Management (TQM), and many other efficiency processes are being employed by countless companies to find Shortcuts. The black belts of Six Sigma are the icons of this process improvement movement; but wise people don't wait for one of these programs to be adopted by their companies. They keep the process going on a daily basis in their own jobs. They ask themselves how they can make every step of their job easier, faster, and more efficient.

Improve just one thing you do in your job every week, and you'll be astounded at how much more efficient and effective you become. It could be anything from how you order supplies to how you organize your hundreds of daily emails. It could be finding a way to better communicate what your department needs to accomplish, or a more efficient process for amassing quarterly numbers for a budget meeting. You might dig into the whole world of one of the biggest perceived time-wasters—meetings. In doing so, you might develop a method that includes only the people who will have real input into the agenda of each meeting, while at the same time discovering a way to transmit the findings of meetings to those who are not present at them. There are so many ways you can continually tinker with all of the tasks of your job, thereby freeing up more time to get at the really juicy stuff—like the priorities of the business.

I work with many physicians and their practices. One of the major complaints of doctors is the time they must spend doing things other than practicing medicine. One physician points out that if a medical staff professional were designated to call all the patients who have normal lab values, this would increase the face-to-face time the doctor would have with patients by up to 60 minutes a day. That's substantial when you consider how much better you feel when you have even five more minutes with your doctor. Shortcuts look for ways to do more of what they do and, in doing so, help others do more of what they do.

Ask your fellow colleagues how much time they actually spend at work. You will typically hear 8 to 10 hours a day. But that's not the point here. When you ask, "How much time do you spend doing the things that are a big payoff to the bottom line?" the answers are startlingly different. To this question you will hear, "two to three hours a day, maximum." That means there are several things they are either not delegating nor finding a faster, easier, and more efficient way to get done; or several tasks they are doing that they should not be doing at all.

At the end of the 1980s and into the 1990s, heavyweight CEO Jack Welch of GE introduced a process called "Work Out." Its sole purpose was to have every employee look at what they do every day and ask, "Should I even be doing this? Is there a better way? Is this something that was valuable to do 10 years ago when it was introduced, but has outlived its usefulness?" Mr. Welch was getting at the very core of what it means to be an intelligent Shortcut on a continual basis. By doing so, GE became one of the most tightly managed, most often emulated, and most admired companies in the world.

I heard a supply chain management consultant talk about how the efficiency of the supply chain can save a company millions of dollars and create the professional image that those organizations want their consumers to instantly associate with them. He says that for a retailer like Best Buy or Circuit City, saving just 30 seconds per cash register transaction adds up to millions of dollars, and helps these companies process more transactions per day, which brings in millions more. The consultant's job, along with other supply chain Shortcuts, is to become so intimate with the process—so expert at understanding how it works—that trimming needless movement and adding productive steps is a worldwide business worth billions, if not trillions.

Shortcut Lesson

When you get really good at something, you can find the efficiencies that save you and others time. Since most are looking to find more time, you become the Shortcut to that goal. Your value goes up.

Organize Your Info

> Information is a source of learning. But unless it is
> organized, processed, and available to the right people,
> in a format for decision making, it is a burden, not a
> benefit.
>
> —WILLIAM POLLARD
> *author,* The Soul of the Firm
> *and chairman of the ServiceMaster Company*

It seemed like an aside when John Naisbitt said it in 1993, in a speech I heard him give about the predictions in his and Patricia Aburdene's book, *Megatrends 2000.*[5] He said, "The most successful people of the twenty-first century will be those who can take the proliferation of information and make sense of it for other people." Truer words were never spoken.

Since the Internet was made available to the public in 1994, information replication has become a major issue. It's said that scientific and technological information is doubling every six to eight years. Compare that to the half-life of your college education, which is about two years. After that, much of the current affairs and technological information you learned becomes obsolete. Here are some other mind-blowing factoids from the world of data overload: A petabyte equals 1 million gigabytes. Downloaded now on a high-speed Internet connection, the last bytes of 1 petabyte would be transferred in the year 2514. It's estimated that Google has 20 petabytes already stored, and as much as 200 petabytes of storage space available.

Now consider this: At the time of this writing, there were more than 130 million items on about 530 miles of bookshelves in the world's largest library: the Library of Congress, in Washington, DC. Imagine the last road trip you took that required more than eight hours of driving, and you'll have driven roughly from one point of information to the other in the Library of Congress. And to increase your breathing rate even further, ponder this: that's nearly 3 million feet on the shelves of the Library of Congress—which doesn't include books and resources digitally archived. If you could read a stack of those books a day—the stack being 10 feet high (about the average floor-to-ceiling distance in an American home), and each book was an average of 2 inches thick, you would have to read 60 books *every day* for about 822 years just to get through the ones already written. And keep in mind, some 125,000 new titles are added every year—and *don't* include the enormous number of volumes of journals and magazines put out each day every year. Go into any large bookstore and you'll see an entire section filled with up to 20 different magazines just on renovating and building kitchens and baths—new every month.

No wonder it's mind-boggling when you're trying to find that one piece of information buried in the haystack of information. What's more, from the time you wake up in the morning to the time you eat dinner, you are exposed to more information than an individual from the medieval period was exposed to in an *entire* lifetime. There is more information in a Sunday edition of the *New York Times* than our ancestors saw—ever. Overwhelmed yet? So is everyone else in the modern world. That's why we need excellent, reliable Shortcuts to help us to cope, survive, and thrive. And that's why if you are one, you are valuable beyond your wildest dreams.

What do we do with all of this information? How are we supposed to stay on top of all the things that make us better at what we do? After all, new information is just a signal to change. Organizations and individuals who come up with a way to classify the information in a way that makes it easier for others to avail themselves of it and use it will be the billion-dollar winners in our world.

Take Google, for example. The word "Google" has become synonymous with searching for information on the Internet. Google began as a college dorm "toy" and morphed into a computer search engine that brings billions of pages of content to users in a matter of seconds. The originators of Google figured out a way to systematize all of the information it now offers—and it pays off in billions of dollars.

Similarly, sites like Expedia and Orbitz are the "Googles" of the travel industry. Amazon.com has vast power because it's the place where so many go, worldwide, to buy books and other items online. iTunes organized the music world; and as of this writing, it's the largest music retailer in the world. It only took a few years to achieve, and all because of a little music organizing gizmo called the iPod.

Even traditional retailers are getting into the one-stop-shop mentality that is revolutionizing how we organize our lives. Shop at a Super Target or Wal-Mart and you can probably find 70 percent of the things you need to buy for everyday use. Bed, Bath and Beyond organizes everything on the home front. The Container Store provides the Shortcuts that organize the everyday clutter of our lives.

Ask yourself: "What area of the chaotic world am I organizing?"

Shortcut Lesson

Figure out a better way to pull data together more usefully; discover how to communicate it to a broad audience; finally, make it easily accessible. The result will be a profitable venture.

Unload the Overload

One of the effects of living with electronic information is that we live habitually in a state of information overload. There's always more than you can cope with.

—MARSHALL MCLUHAN
social reformer

The other thing all of this information leads to is overload and paralysis. We all need people who can become our Shortcuts in a variety of different areas of our lives. We have to have these go-to people so that we have the time to become great Shortcuts ourselves. If you're not using a lot of Shortcuts, it is highly unlikely that you'll be a great Shortcut for others. You simply won't have the time. Great Shortcuts free up time to do the things about which they are passionate and for which they wish to become a world-class Shortcut. They do this by finding others who can take things off their plates.

In his autobiography *Jack: Straight from the Gut,*[6] Jack Welch talks about many of the philosophies that influenced him to become the Goliath business leader that he was. One that stands out in particular is Peter Drucker's management idea of "back-room" and "front-room" activities.[7] In essence, if something is not your front-room activity, find someone for whom it is and let that person do it. For GE, front-room activities include making aircraft engines, power turbines, and medical equipment. Advertising is not a front-room activity, so it doesn't produce advertising, even though the company needs it. Instead, GE finds companies for which advertising is a front-room activity and lets them be a Shortcut. GE nurtures these companies like crazy and treats them as one of the family; but the company does not confuse itself by doing things that are not aspects of its front-room activities.

Great Shortcuts do the same. They look at all they need to be successful in life, and systematically create a list of those requirements. Then they circle those that are front-room activities and put them to the side. When you're growing as a Shortcut, your main focus is to make sure you have all of your back-room activities taken care of and nurtured. The other thing you want to be clear about is what your front-room activities truly are. It might serve you well to look at all aspects of your life and keep track of the things that you do yourself. Can some of those things be given to a Shortcut for whom it would be a front-room activity? It's understood that sometimes a housekeeper or a lawn service doesn't fit the budget; but look very closely and make deliberate decisions about what you're doing. You're attempting to free up time to spend on your true front-room activities. My list of back-room activities looks like this (my front-room activities are incredibly few):

Personal

Housecleaning: Trish

Lawn service: Beautiful Lawn Landscapers

Gutters: Denver Gutters

Dog sitter: Camp Bow Wow

Car service: Steve Saykally

Car wash: Finish Line Car Wash

Professional

Editor: Becky

Web administrator: Taa

Project manager: Stacy

Client manager: Marci

Business development: Marty

Printing: Mary Ann

Audio and video duplication: Mary Ann

Exercise

Who are your shortcuts?	What for?
1.	
2.	
3.	
4.	
5.	
6.	
7.	

Make your own personal and professional lists and insert the names of people who do these things for you. If you do them for yourself, ask if it is time for you to find someone else to do them for you. Start out small if your budget doesn't allow another big expenditure. For example, if you want to give up major housekeeping chores, hire someone to come in once a month. As your budget permits, increase the frequency. My guess is that you will find a way to make it work, because the time you get back is well worth the extra dollars you spend.

As you look at your list, ask yourself about the Shortcuts you use. When was the last time you reached out and acknowledged those people, and made them feel like a part of the family? More on this later; but, remember, those Shortcuts give you more time and space to be an excellent Shortcut yourself.

Shortcut Lesson

To be a Shortcut, you have to use Shortcuts. The sphere of people who support your life and make it work for you should be deliberately and carefully chosen. Those you choose will be people who are sometimes friends, sometimes colleagues, and always those who are experts in their own specific areas.

Scoop It Up

Shortcuts Are in All Types of Careers

> They're with me all the time. They're with me when I go
> in. They're with me when I come out. They're with me
> when I take a nap. They're there when my dog poops.
> —SHIRLEY MacLAINE
> *actress and author*

Shortcuts can be found in all walks of life and at every level of an organization. You don't have to have an important title or a glamorous job. In fact, often it seems that the less people want to do a required chore, the more they're willing to pay someone else to do it. Shortcuts view it as their duty to do the best job in their particular field. *DoodyCalls* is an example of a Shortcut that has figured out this important formula.

DoodyCalls is a Virginia-based dog poop-scooping company started by Jacob and Susan D'Aniello, in 2000. It's now a franchisor bringing in a start-up fee of around $25,000 per franchise, and growing at a rate that would make any small business owner bay at the moon. The company specializes in doing one thing well, and gets paid handsomely for it. It has been featured in *USA Today,* the *Washington Post,* and several other newspapers of note. The simplicity and clarity of the service it offers seem to capture the imaginations of readers—that, and the fact that the company is making its franchise owners millionaires by doing something others could but don't want to do.

DoodyCalls is the perfect Shortcut. It takes care of an essential element of life—picking up after our pets. Its poop-scoopers do so with stealth. They're in, they're out, they're consistent, and they have a good attitude. Customers are grateful to write the weekly check. All I want to know is, when is one opening in my neighborhood?!

In a somewhat similar role is June Dahms, a collector for a credit union. She loves making those phone calls that most of us would dread. She's great at it and, frankly, not many people in her company would be as adept at making people feel good about having a collector call. June says most people actually want to figure out a way to pay, but they become afraid because they don't understand their options. June makes these people feel responsible again, by giving them a way to pay down their debt. In the meantime, the credit union gets its due. She's a Shortcut doing what a lot of people would fail at; she's so good at it that she also helps other collectors avoid getting angry at the people who owe them money, thereby preventing a major public relations nightmare. There's artistry to being a Shortcut at the things most people don't want to do.

You can probably think of, and actually might already be in, a career like this. The more you are willing to become an expert at something no one else wants to do—and do it with a great attitude— the more influential and valuable you become.

Shortcut Lesson

It doesn't matter what you choose to do in life. If you do it exceedingly well, you'll be a Shortcut. If you do it exceedingly well and it's something others don't want to do, you'll be a rich Shortcut.

The Washed-Up Shortcut

What Have You Done for Me Lately?

> A style does not go out of style as long as it adapts
> itself to its period. When there is an incompatibility
> between the style and a certain state of mind, it is never
> the style that triumphs.
>
> —Coco Chanel
> *French fashion designer*

We all have heard stories of people who came up with a brilliant, cost-saving product or marketing idea, and made their companies a lot of dough. Subsequently, they ride on the reputation of that innovation for a long time, until wham! Someone at the top starts looking at the top-heavy salary of this innovator—who, naturally, got his cushy job as a reward for his find. But now this has-been's mid-six-figure income has come screaming off the page. The top executive asks what this person has done for the company lately. She is incensed to find out that Mister Brainiac has been riding this bubble for a number of years now. Demands are made of him to justify his salary, but he has done nothing since. He's no longer sharp. He's been taking long lunches, advantage of the perks—and the company for a long ride.

Who can blame this guy and his ilk for playing out the fame and fortune thing for a while? All too often such people are allowed to hang out in the deep, dark cracks of the ivory tower, to be found there only when a very sharp pencil poking around digs them out of it. When that's done, these folks have a few years, at the very most, to perform. Some do. Some do not. They head into retirement or off to look for another job (based on their 25-year-old innovation). Hopefully, they have not spent all of their big income. They're going to need it.

Shortcut Lesson

Even at the very top, you have to be a Shortcut, for the street, to investors, to the board of directors, to your mother. People often look at CEOs and wonder why they are so driven. It is because they know the road to long-lasting success lies in being or finding the next Shortcut. They live for it. They look for it. And when they find it, they are on to the next one, because this latest, greatest Shortcut they just found is already yesterday's news.

Raise Your Hand

How to Be Counted as a Shortcut

> An expert is someone who knows some of the worst
> mistakes that can be made in his subject, and how to
> avoid them.
>
> —WERNER KARL HEISENBERG
> *German physicist*

Approximately 70 percent of high-functioning professionals suffer from what is called fraud or impostor syndrome, according to organizational psychologist Manfred F. R. Kets de Vries.[8] In other words, many of us are scared to death that others will find out we don't know what they think we know. If you have this syndrome, it means that no matter whether you're degreed and/or pedigreed, you still can't believe you deserve the influence, accolades, and rewards that come with what you do. As a result, you might spend an excessive amount of time and energy making sure others don't see what you don't know, or don't think you know; or you might go to the other extreme, attempting to demonstrate that you do know what you're talking about, by showing off.

Such an outlook is understandable in a world where being right seems to have a premium on it. But Shortcuts know they can't be all things to all people, so they figure out the one thing they do well. They know the area in which they are pros. For which part of your job would you raise your hand to say, "pick me; I can do that," if the stakes were high and the need for success was too? Think about that as you read through the following scenario.

You've been invited to "sit at the table"—that is, with the most influential decision makers in your organization. They don't know you or your abilities, but someone thinks enough of you to have invited you to attend the meeting. Maybe your presence is seen as an opportunity for you to learn something from the big dogs, and you're really not expected to participate; in which case, you'll be introduced and quickly acknowledged. But the overriding purpose of the meeting is to discuss something that is regarded as beyond your experience or knowledge, so you are just expected to listen.

As the meeting goes on, the CEO begins to look frustrated. She wants this issue solved, but so far no one in the room has offered the insight she needs to put this problem to bed. You sheepishly raise your hand. The others in the room audibly gasp, while glancing sideways at one another. Who is this person? Why is he raising his hand? What audacity! You're aware of the response, but you forge ahead anyway. You begin by admitting you don't know everything about this issue, but that you do believe you are the best person to address the database aspect of it—which seems to be one of the main sticking points in resolving the problem. This area, you tell the group modestly but confidently, is where you're an expert, where you spend extra time staying up to date. You are the Shortcut for this. "I can do it," you state assuredly.

If that were you in this scenario, at what point in the meeting would you have raised your hand to say "pick me!"? The answer to that question will tell you how you view yourself as a Shortcut—the pro.

No question, it's easy to get bogged down during each day among all the different tasks you are involved in. But it's essential to figure out those you really excel at. Think about what you know hands-down, which job you are confident you can do as well or better than others. This takes courage, to be sure. But think about it: someone is going to be selected to do the job; it might as well be you. So raise your hand and assert yourself. Remember, as a self-aware Shortcut, you create your own future.

Exercise

If you are unsure of the expertise you bring to the table, or you are unable to articulate it to yourself, try this: Find five people who know your work and whose honest opinion you value. Ask each of them: What is the one skill or task at which they believe you excel? Ask for specifics. They might not be able to articulate their thoughts well either, but if they describe a detailed scenario, you'll be able to mine their responses for the insight you need.

This takes both courage and grace. Preface your request like this: "I have a favor to ask. I'm reading a book about becoming influential and understanding my particular strengths. You've worked with me a lot. If you had to specify just one strength I've displayed that you think brings value to you or the organization, what would it be?" You might want to give them some time to think about it and get back to you later, but I prefer the more immediate, instinctive response, because I believe it's usually more accurate.

Shortcut Lesson

No one can do it all, but each of us can do a few things extraordinarily well. Become a self-aware Shortcut; figure out your skills and polish them to brilliance. When you do, you'll have no problem raising your hand when the occasion calls for it.

Get Some Screen Time

Put Your Money Where the Shortcut Is

Simplicity is the ultimate sophistication.
—Leonardo da Vinci

The folks at software companies hire code writers who typically have wonderfully wry senses of humor. Somewhere in their software, they often embed fun little items that most of us never see. For example, in one piece of software, when users clicked on the About . . . link and then did a Control-click on that page, they would see a credit listing of all the people who had worked on the software design, complete with music and dancing bears—a fun, harmless feature that, thank goodness, users didn't have to pay for. Unfortunately, there are too many products out there that have irrelevant and/or useless features for which we do have to pay, and which we would rather the companies eliminate or cut the cost of the products. Better yet, why don't these companies spend their efforts developing something we really can use?

When I was a television news producer and writer in the eighties, it was easy to get caught up in all of the technological advances that were rapidly changing electronic media. The president of our station, Roger Ogden, was arguably one of the most respected and revered anywhere in the television business, worldwide. He had a sixth sense about what would make a station great. One of the things for which he became known was his ability to spend money that would "end up on the screen." In other words, if someone asked the station to buy equipment, get involved in a community event, or hire certain personnel, Roger would make his decision about whether it was a good spend by judging how much of it would end up on a viewer's screen. That, in his mind, was the ultimate point of the business we were in—the one that put things on the screen of a viewer, our consumer. Roger excelled at keeping everyone on the same page because he always brought us back to basics.

Back to basics: it's a relatively simple acid-test that many individuals and organizations forget as they begin to add frills to their offerings. Ask: Is your frill ending up "on the screen" of your customers or your boss? Shortcuts make sure that all they do doesn't get in the way of their primary offering.

One frill that seems to have escaped this basic scrutiny comes to mind: airplane food. It seemed to take forever for the airline industry to conduct a survey, which told them that the majority of travelers would rather not eat their food. In fact, they learned, serving food on domestic flights created more hassle and bad attitude than it was worth. But most airlines learned this only after the whole darned industry nearly went belly up! Sure, the flying public got used to the Shortcut of having food provided on board, but once most airlines did away with the service, people figured out on their own how to fill their bellies before or during their flights. Other Shortcuts cropped up in airports—namely, restaurants that created take-on-board packs of food.

Vickie, a senior executive of a multibillion-dollar firm told me of one of her employees, Stan, who provided her with an extra PowerPoint presentation that didn't really offer value. When she heard the discussion about this in my workshop, she decided to approach Stan about it. She asked him why he always included a PowerPoint deck with every report he produced for her. Stan replied, "I just always thought it was something you could use. And since I'm pretty good at working with PowerPoint, it's really not that much more for me to do that for you."

Vickie realized this was clearly a Shortcut that didn't "hit the screen." So she told Stan, "You provide everything I need in the financial reports for the executive committee. But I would rather have them earlier than have to wait for the PowerPoint deck you include. I really don't need the deck for the reports I give, and I know you're putting a lot of time and energy into doing this." Though Stan was discouraged initially, Vickie dispelled it quickly, by reminding him his value overall was immeasurable.

Shortcut Lesson

Shortcuts get back to basics, by asking on a regular basis, "What are we really doing here? Does the extra frill add to my value or distract me from being a Shortcut?" Ask the questions, and the answers may surprise you. You might find they're not actually Shortcuts, for the masses, your customers, or your boss. Put your money where the Shortcuts can be seen and felt by your customer—"on the screen."

Rule the Rules

The rule which forbids ending a sentence with a preposition is the kind of nonsense up with which I will not put.

—WINSTON CHURCHILL

Do you ever get frustrated when you are fed a rule that does not make sense to you? Think about when you return an item, come up against a work policy, or try to change your airline ticket, and the customer service representative neatly recites the applicable rule and points to the fine print, which you were supposed to be able to read. It is maddening.

The funny thing is that if you ask customer service reps why a specific, seemingly needless rule is being applied, most of the time they can't give you an answer. Here's a rule of thumb for this Shortcut about rules: Shortcuts don't get bogged down in rules and procedures that impede forward progress. They understand the spirit and intent of a policy and its rules. Shortcuts understand that their role is not to teach customers how to behave properly according to the rules, but to delight the customer while getting them what they need. If you or your organization has rules, and your customer service people can't explain them or they don't understand the spirit of the rule, don't expect the customer experience to be even close to a good one. Thus, you are in danger of becoming a bottleneck.

A few years ago, a client bought me a business-class ticket to Europe on the airline I fly most often. It cost a large amount of money, by anyone's standards. My client asked me to book it myself, and so I looked for the lowest fare possible—which was still very, very expensive. Fortunately, I had special worldwide upgrades accumulated from my frequent travel with the airline, and I thought it would be a good time to use the upgrades and experience what it felt like to sit in one of those first-class seats that lie flat. I learned I had to purchase the ticket before I could apply the upgrade. I did so, then discovered the online system wouldn't let me upgrade my flight *to* Europe, only *from* Europe. I phoned the special customer service desk for 100,000-mile fliers. In retrospect, I admit I should have waited to do this, because I was sporting a horrible head cold and was not in the mood for airline-rule shenanigans. It didn't help that when I talked to the service representative she was at a loss as to why the upgrade wouldn't work for the outbound flight. Finally, she saw it.

"Mr. Halford, here it is," she said. "Your flight from Denver to Dulles is a *Y* fare and the one from Dulles to Geneva is a *Z* fare. It needs to be a *C* fare." She stated all this in a tone that made it sound as if that should explain everything.

I retorted, "And I should know that because . . . ?" To which she said, "It's published in the fare rules." Then she began to lecture (or so it seemed to me) in a rather pert manner, that I hadn't spent enough money on the outbound part of my fare to warrant being able to use my gift from the airline without exceptions being applied. There are rules, I was further informed, about when that upgrade may be used as well, even though it was flaunted as a perk for the airline's regular travelers.

I doubt her aim was to provoke me, but nevertheless, I was. I asked her, in a testy tone, how I should have known about all of these rules, and how I could avoid being a "bad" customer in the future. Of course, my insolence didn't improve her attitude any. She said if I would just look at the fare rules, I would see this. (If you have ever purchased an international airline ticket, you know that it comes laden with many restrictions, which read like a book on regulatory statutes for dealing with some obscure element of the law.)

I next asked her if these made any sense to her, to which she offered up dead silence—eventually followed by the inevitable question, was there anything else she could help me with. Just for the sport of it, I decided to see if she would engage with me a bit more on the rules. I asked if she could imagine the discussion during which this set of rules was decided. She told me she did not know what my point was. I said, "You can't seem to explain to me why there are rules like this, much less explain what the rules are without simply reciting them to me from a computer screen. I think your company has put you at a disadvantage, resulting in irritated customers like me. And I want to know why." Feeling particularly cantankerous, I continued: "And you are your airline's top-tier service provider. How on earth do your regular service representatives come close to dealing with these inane rules with less savvy travelers?"

She had had enough, clearly, but she was well enough trained not to hang up on me; but she did begin to address me as if I were a third grader, saying, "What are you asking, sir?" I shot back, "I'm asking, do I need a college degree in how to be this airline's customer in order to have a pleasant experience? I know you can't answer that, and all I ask you to do is to relate this conversation to anyone who actually cares about the future of your airline. Thank you for listening." I was fuming.

The airline business is a tough one, with customers wanting to know the whys and wherefores. And that's where there is such an enormous opportunity to differentiate one airline from the next. If more airlines would pay attention to the numbers of obstacles that have been created to the flying public, and at least answer *why*, more of their customers would probably report at least having had a satisfactory experience, instead of the abysmal one most associate with the airlines in recent years. It would cut down on ridiculous temper tantrums like the one I had, as well.

One of the most powerful words in the English language is "because." Harvard professor Ellen Langer's career in psychology has centered on mindfulness and control. Her study about controlling outcomes by giving reasons for favors and rules is fascinating.[9]

In its most basic sense, the study shows that adding a mindful "because" to describe why you want a favor, or to explain some seemingly inappropriate rule, gives you much greater control over the outcome. When you can offer someone a sensible "because," you prevent a lot of headaches, for you and your organization. We all just want to know *why* sometimes. If your employees can't answer that, either teach them the "because," or eliminate the relevant barrier to doing business.

Shortcut Lesson

The question is yours to answer: Is the Shortcut you are providing worth all of the rules you impose on it?

Become the Master

When you have worked well, there should be no sign
that you have worked at all.

—GERALDINE BROOKS
Pulitzer Prize–winning author of
People of the Book, *Viking Press, 2008*

What we must decide is perhaps how we are valuable
rather than how valuable we are.

—EDGAR Z. FRIEDENBERG
sociologist and professor

The world today is a very noisy place. It's characterized by chaos and constant, rapid change. It is a very different place from when Leonardo da Vinci, Michelangelo, Donatello, and their contemporaries graced the planet. These masters had a more wide-open palette on which to create and awe the world with their brilliance.

Is their level of genius still present on this planet? The answer has to be yes; but, undoubtedly, it is more difficult to recognize because of all the noise and distractions. The achievers in today's world typically rise above the chaos and cast themselves as masters within a much smaller niche of expertise than those of yesteryear. This is counterintuitive to the generalist mentality embraced by modern culture. There are a lot of people who do a lot of things, but fewer people who do a few things exceptionally well. They are the masters. They are the ultimate Shortcuts, because they are the ones we go to as our definitive resources in the world. That makes them worth a lot of money and gives them considerable influence.

So who are the modern masters, and what do they have in common? The most recognizable ones are those who are showcased in the media—on the Web, in popular magazines, in the news, or on television. Think: Oprah Winfrey, Bill Gates, Warren Buffett, Barbra Streisand, Jack Welch, and Meg Whitman, even Simon Cowell and his crew of *American Idol* colleagues. These are all big names and fit the criterion for mastery (which I'll reveal to you in a moment). But most of us—though we may respect some or all of these people greatly—can't see ourselves attaining their kind of fame and fortune. "If that's what mastery is about," you might think, "then it's not going to happen to me in this lifetime."

Mastery is a simple idea. It's not a destination, but a life-long process; and somewhere on the road to it, people start to sit up and take notice that you have a few more skills and polished expertise than the average bear. The simplest way I've heard mastery described is as *someone who is in full command of a subject.* It doesn't mean he or she knows everything about it; it means he or she has studied it and worked in and with it enough to grasp those questions that are still unanswered in the field, who can think new thoughts about it, and who are essentially Shortcuts to the information and application of that topic.

To that definition, then, it is possible to add many names in many career paths, in all spheres of your life. There are janitors, CEOs, administrators, salespeople, auto mechanics, service people of every kind, academicians, physicians, nurses, medical assistants, engineers, lawyers, payroll clerks—and the list goes on and on. In the following pages, you'll meet some of my Shortcuts that I consider masters in their fields. As you read, I encourage you to think about where you are in the world of mastery. "Raise Your Hand," the Shortcut described earlier, is a good way to jump-start this process.

Here's one of mine: Cara Tracy. The world could be crumbling down around someone and you would never know it if Cara were in charge. She is the vice president of professional development for the National Speakers' Association. It's an organization that caters to and educates—you guessed it—professional speakers, worldwide. As you might imagine, this group is difficult to plan a major meeting for—speakers are in the business, after all. Yet, year after year, Cara and her incredible group of masters in the meeting department pull off a dazzling industry convention that tops the previous one. She carries around an eight-pound notebook, and wears a headset into which she's being given directions to go right and left and up and down, seemingly simultaneously; and she carries it off with a smile, all the while paying courteous attention to large numbers of people with diverse needs. And no one would ever know, for example, that the stage fell apart 30 minutes before the general session. She doesn't deem that to be anyone's problem but her own, and her crew's. She's a master—and I believe Leonardo would count her in those ranks. You can be one, too.

Shortcuts are experts in their own "fiefdoms." They own their little corner of the world. They know it so well that they become *the* go-to resource. You wouldn't think of going anywhere else. When you say of someone, "They're expensive, but they're worth it," you're describing a Shortcut who has achieved mastery, whether you're talking about a plumber or a neurosurgeon.

Fortunately, we were all born prewired for certain strengths, which can lead to mastery; indeed, we sucked in this capability with our first glorious lungsful of oxygen. Martin E. P. Seligman, PhD, the founder of an area of psychology called "positive psychology," delves into what is right and good about people, instead of focusing on what is wrong with them and how to fix it. His body of research brings about an entirely different look at how to make people "whole," as well as how to help them to excel. Seligman, and his colleague Christopher Peterson, PhD, defined more than 20 areas of strength that will help individuals excel, if applied in earnest, among them gratitude, the appreciation of beauty and excellence, prudence, love of learning, creativity, and critical thinking.[10, 20]

Similarly, Marcus Buckingham and Donald Clifton, PhD detailed their own set of strengths in their best-selling book *Now, Discover Your Strengths.*[11] Their definitions of strengths map very closely with those of Seligman and Peterson; they just call them something different. Buckingham and Clifton incited a revolution in corporations around the world by suggesting the seemingly avant-garde idea that if a company focuses on the strengths of the individual, the whole organization will be better as a result. That seems like nothing more than common sense, but it upset the more rule-bound job descriptions upon which most organizations are built. Think about it: Most of work life is like a complicated cake recipe, from whose ingredients you are told *never* to vary, if you wish to bake the perfect cake. But aren't we all secretly envious of that rebel who takes a supposedly tried-and-true recipe, adds a little of this and a little of that, to create a one-of-a-kind cake? That same thing can happen for you, if you're willing to veer off-course a bit, experiment, and find out more about what it is that really tickles your tummy.

The point of this discussion is not new. Shortcuts have known about strengths for centuries. They were drawn to and spent their lives developing those strengths. Corporations are just now coming around to the fact that when people like what they're doing and excel at their tasks, the result is a more powerful organization. It is a simple but often-ignored universal law.

All that said, the real work begins only after you discover your strengths. *The process to become a master, a Shortcut extraordinaire, is not a Shortcut in itself.* It takes time and focus. It takes dedication and discipline. Ironically, this is good news for those who set this as their goal, because there are few people who are willing to put in the time it takes to bolster their strengths and achieve mastery. Ironically, in fact, many people instead work on their weaknesses, whether they realize it or not—because that's what they've been taught to do all of their lives. Think about spelling tests, where the focus was always on how many words you misspelled—not how many you got right. That approach is, simply, counterproductive.

Don't misinterpret what I'm saying here, however: A weakness is a weakness when it becomes a liability, and gets in your way to success. If, say, you are not adept at piano playing but you don't need that skill for the life you're leading, then it's not a weakness. If, on the other hand, you're a music major in college, and you can't play at least basic piano, then it is a weakness. To overcome or improve upon an area of weakness, it is necessary to put in some time to learn new skills and behaviors. The majority of people who work on their liabilities become competent; that is to say, they become average, or mediocre, in these areas. And for many purposes, that is okay. When that is where all of your focus goes, however, you're not putting in due diligence on the areas of strength that will set you apart. True mastery comes when you discover your heritable strengths and begin to work on them as intensely as you might on those weaknesses. When you take the time to develop and use your signature capabilities, there is a good chance you will soar above others, because your strength might be their weakness.

I learned this lesson the hard way. During my freshman year of college, I was privileged to take advanced writing, because I excelled at English and writing in high school. So there I was, the only freshman in the advanced writing class of only 16 students. Dr. Wagner, our professor, was a wonderfully warm, wise, maternal woman who had taught thousands of students over the years. She had been an assistant to Ernest Hemingway, so it was a true honor to learn from her.

Each week, our assignment was to write a paper. There were a total of seven essays, plus the final paper. Dr. Wagner would make extensive critical, but encouraging, notes on all of our weekly papers. She was always glowing in her comments about my writing. Now remember: I was a self-satisfied, egotistical teenager at the time, and my self-image bloated further after reading her comments. She gave us no grade, just comments. The final grade would come after she assessed our improvement over the semester.

My final paper came back with her comments, on which Dr. Wagner again praised my writing. She told me I could blossom into a great and creative writer; but for my efforts and ability, she wrote, "I have to give you a 'D,' and it's about your desire." A D for desire! I couldn't believe it. I was there on partial academic scholarship and this grade would definitely jeopardize that. I was furious, especially in light of what she wrote on each of my papers—and given my high opinion of myself.

I tried to get an audience with her, with no luck. I went to university officials who reviewed my case and said that Dr. Wagner was well within her rights—and that she was the only person who could change my grade. But, she wouldn't meet with me! I didn't even tell my parents because I was so mortified at the thought that anyone would think me less than perfect.

Finally, at the end of the next semester, she agreed to meet with me. I was loaded for bear! I had all of my papers from class with me. I sat down in front of her desk and began making demands, while she listened respectfully. When I was finished with my diatribe, she said, "Scott, stop me when I'm wrong. About an hour to an hour and a half before class, you sit down at the typewriter and write your first and final draft."

I told her, with no small degree of pride and smugness—and not knowing what point she was trying to prove—that she was right.

She continued, "And, your writing is quite good. Imagine what it would be like if you took the time that others take who are less gifted. Scott, this writing, this ability to communicate is a gift. Your 'D' is reflective of your abilities in relation to your output. These papers are *your* 'D' work. Your 'A' work would look very different than these papers, and if you took the time to really read my comments on your papers, you would see that I was strongly pushing you to do more. I will not be a party to anyone wasting a gift, and that's what you're doing."

She didn't change the grade. I was angry for years afterward, until I grew up, my ego grew down, and I saw the wisdom and truth in her lesson. If we have a gift, we should work harder on improving and refining it. We should take even more time to develop our skills or talent. We shouldn't go on "cruise control" just because we're better at something than someone else. Her wisdom remains with me to this day, and I know I'll remember her throughout my life as the first person to truly teach me about mastery.

According to gurus on the topic, strengths have some attributes in common, when they're being used:

- People typically excel at things they enjoy.

- They are happier, feel more energy, and even more joy while they're using, and after they use, their strength.

- They perform at higher skill levels for longer periods of time (more on this in the next chapter). They behave like excellent Shortcuts. If you take a stab at mastery, you will, too.

- People working with their strengths have a tendency to rapidly learn the skills associated with those strengths.

- They also tend to want to keep on learning more deeply about their strength or the topic area in which their strength is being used.

- They become good teachers around the strength, and want to show others how they can benefit from it.

- Others feel good around a person who is practicing his or her strength. They might actually cheer that person on because he or she is seemingly perfection in motion.

When you recognize your signature strengths, you can work to enhance them. They can show up in many different vocations that you might choose. The ultimate mastery, however, is when your strength is most closely matched to what you do. For example, consider that one of the strengths Seligman and Peterson list is the appreciation of beauty and excellence. This is evident in someone who loves to be in the presence of people and things they consider excellent. Someone who has this strength could find several ways—in any work setting—to use it. For an obvious example think about someone who works in a performance or aesthetic field—they would have the opportunity to really develop this strength area. Maybe less evident, but still able to employ the strength of appreciation and beauty are a football coach, a teacher, a museum curator, even a house cleaner. If you love what you do, and become highly skilled at it, you will be greatly recognized for your contributions, and typically be highly valued, as well.

A master in any vocation can just as easily be an administrator, daycare worker, executive leader, marketing professional, salesperson, hotel maid, chef, and so on. There is no limit to the areas in which you can perform your mastery. And when you do, others will notice. They will go to you because you are the very best resource they've encountered for that skill. They will keep coming back because they get all the benefits that a Shortcut bestows on their lucky recipients: efficiency, energy, good attitude, and quality.

In a workshop I led on becoming a Shortcut, one person asked if being a Shortcut might be overblown. She said that she was an excellent Shortcut, and her colleagues would attest to that. She also said that because she was recognized as *the* resource, she was overwhelmed by the number of people who leaned on her.

A couple of things came to mind. First, that's such a nice problem to have. The opposite situation is certainly not enviable and not valued. Second, it sounded to me as if she could negotiate for more money; maybe a different position that granted her greater autonomy and decision making power around her availability; any number of things that she might wish for to keep her from being overused. She was in the bargaining seat because of her dedication to her mastery. If she truly was a Shortcut with both mastery and emotional intelligence, her influence would be extremely high and a discussion with her boss was probably in order.

Shortcut Lesson

Typically, the more mastery you achieve, the rarer you and your talents become; and with that, the more valuable you become. You are a unique gem. Do not ignore your strengths. It's where you'll find mastery. The rest will probably lead to mediocre abilities. If you find yourself in the situation where you're overworked, and it is indeed true that you are *the* resource, it's time to negotiate. Mastery has its privileges, but sometimes you have to ask for them. Make sure, however, before you negotiate, that you read through the chapters on know-how. Expertise accounts for only a portion of what makes a Shortcut a Shortcut. If you're lacking in know-how, your negotiations might not go as well as you would like.

Find the Flow

Hitting the Zone as a Shortcut

> The difference between what we do and what we are
> capable of doing would suffice to solve most of the
> world's problems.
>
> —Mohandas Gandhi

Another influential psychological researcher in the area of human performance is Mihaly Csikszentmihalyi, who introduced a revolutionary concept while at the University of Chicago. His theory on flow—the study of optimal performance—is key to understanding how to become a master Shortcut.[12]

Csikszentmihalyi first studied people in demanding pastimes that provided no direct obvious reward. He initially chose those who spent a good deal of time in physically and mentally challenging activities, such as amateur athletes and artists, rock climbers, composers, and chess players. He asked them several questions to find out if they had something in common that kept them going at their difficult activity. He discovered that most of these people described their experiences in similar terms. He also discovered that as people stayed "in flow" for longer periods of time, their abilities and enjoyment increased significantly. Later, Csikszentmihalyi interviewed ordinary people to see if the same things could be experienced by mere mortals. The short answer is that indeed they can. These things were universal in his subjects' experiences:

1. They described a sense of timelessness—a feeling that time had become distorted and had caused them to lose track of it altogether. This is particularly interesting in light of the fact that this phenomenon happened with athletes who had

taken part in timed events. Interestingly, the limit on time isn't where their attention is directed when they're performing tasks at the highest levels.

2. The skill felt simple. Another remarkable finding, in light of the fact that the people interviewed were participating in activities that required excellent skill in order to participate at continuous and safe levels.

3. Self-consciousness faded away and the individual concentrated only on the moment at hand. They weren't concerned with a lot of the external forces that can often lead to self-doubt.

4. There was a general sense of euphoria and joy in the person completing the task. It was such a pleasurable sense that the individual would perform it again—even though there was high difficulty and sometimes danger involved.

Csikszentmihalyi labeled this experience "flow," and wrote a book about it, appropriately called, *Flow: The Psychology of Optimal Experience.* He was able to break down the experience into two dimensions: challenge and skill. Say you're a new Ping-Pong player and you find an opponent who is equally inexperienced. You both have low skill, and the challenge is low. You could very well experience a bit of flow—or beginner's luck as it's sometimes called. (See Figure A.)

But this won't last long, because you'll soon decide to find a better opponent. The challenge goes up; but if you don't get instruction and increase your skill, the result might look like that shown in Figure B.

You are out of flow and most likely experiencing anxiety— Mother Nature's signal that it's time to learn more skills to cope. Assuming you get some professional instruction and increase your proficiency, your outcome might look more like Figure C.

You are back in flow. You become very good at the skills you've been taught, but you keep playing with the same opponent, so the challenge doesn't increase. You get out of flow again. (See Figure D.)

Figure A

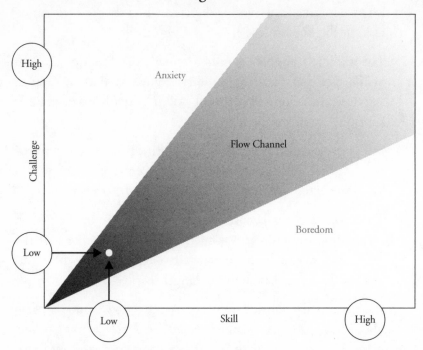

Now you are feeling bored—another emotional signal from Mother Nature that it's time to challenge yourself further in order to get back into the flow channel.

So, essentially, flow is that space lodged between anxiety and boredom. It's a fine balancing act; and it's not to say that we won't feel a good deal of anxiety and/or boredom along the way. Masters don't give up, though. They acknowledge where they are, and are self-aware and disciplined enough to self-correct. The more we work at adding to our challenges while increasing our skills, the longer we stay in flow, and the higher up the flow channel we travel. You can discern from the illustrations shown here that while high challenge and high skill take a good amount of dedication, they also enable the flow channel to widen and the extraordinary feelings

Figure B

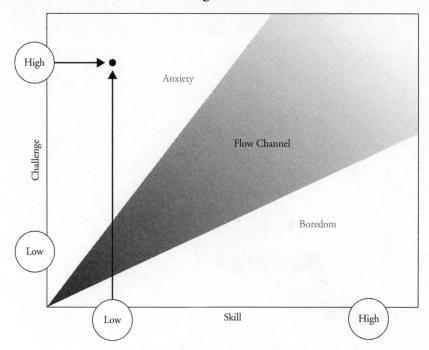

Figure C

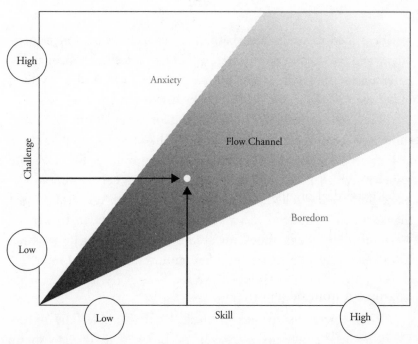

Figure D

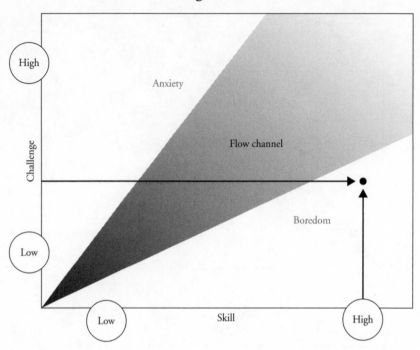

just described to swell. We maintain these feelings for longer periods when we continue to test ourselves. Excellent Shortcuts— entertainers, sports figures, administrators, CEOs, and everything in between—are in flow, or always striving to achieve it.

When you're lacking entertainment or stimulation, do something new or different for 15 minutes. I like to pick up magazines at those big magazine racks that cover every walk of life. I choose topics in which I have absolutely no interest. When I'm on an airplane and feeling bored, I take out the magazine on farm animal management or hot rod cars and thumb through them. It sparks a lot of creativity; I can almost always find something useful to apply to my own life. In a matter of a few minutes, I'm out of my complacent, apathetic, bored-out-of-my-skull state. Try it and see what it brings up for you.

When you're anxious, take a break. It's that simple. The Yerkes-Dodson Law[13] about anxiety tells us to do just that. The law shows us that a little bit of anxiety, or edge—also called "psychic tension"—is good for learning. You learn better if you have that little twinge of apprehension in the back of your mind that says you know you're going to be tested on the information. But, as the Yerkes-Dodson law demonstrates, if the tension is left to its own devices, and allowed to grow unchecked, our abilities fall off rapidly.

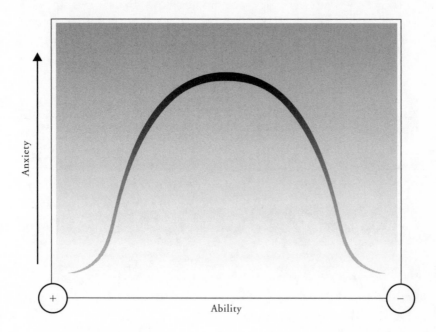

That's when it's time to walk away, take a breather, calm yourself; do something completely different for at least 30 minutes. The distraction will reduce the stress chemicals in your brain and allow you to be more creative. If you're missing data or skills, don't increase your anxiety by pretending you already have what you need. That denial only leads to more intense anxiety and, ultimately, poor performance. It also exacerbates the "fraud" or "impostor" syndrome, which often occurs as you move higher in an organization. This phenomenon manifests when you're met with a challenge for which you don't have the skill or knowledge that you're expected to have. It's the little voice that goes off in your head and says, "Oh no . . . what if they find out I don't know what they think I know?!" It's anxiety-producing and will not give you the performance excellence required at high levels.

Shortcut Lesson

To get to the other side—the side of flow, of feeling accomplished—you must balance between anxiety and boredom. Both states are useful; positive things can happen when you are a little anxious or a little bored. But if you stay in either place for too long, you risk burnout, exhaustion, and discouragement.

Take a break. Get more information or more training. Better yet, get coaching. A good coach will help manage you into flow more quickly than you might be able to yourself. His or her perspective, if you listen to it, can be invaluable. Being a Shortcut is a deliberate act, not one that happens without effort.

Train Your Brain

> I wanted to change the world. But, I found that the only
> thing one can be sure of changing is oneself.
>
> —ALDOUS HUXLEY
> *English novelist*

It takes constant work and change to be a cutting-edge Shortcut. It's not easy, and only the ones who keep working gain the advantage of being the top Shortcut.

Changing one's home address, and all that goes with it, is headache enough to dissuade most of us from doing it too often. Now think about changing your behavior. Multiply the effort it takes to move from one place to another by at least 50 and you will have some idea what it takes to achieve new, lasting positive behavioral habits. This is not intended to discourage you, but rather to encourage you to engage the same mind-set that superstars in any field and at any level take to reach the top.

It's not easy to be excellent; but actually, this is good news for those of you who want to excel. Why? Because most people—including your competitors—won't do what it takes to be excellent. Oh, they'll *say* they want to be top performers, but their actions will rarely be congruent with their words. Shortcut superstars don't give up when the going gets tough. They keep on going—and that is often the major difference between them and those who "could have been."

Keep on reading if you want to learn how to keep on going.

THE CHANGE PROCESS IS BIOLOGICAL

All behavioral change begins as a thought. And it's the desire behind the thought that determines whether the change will stick or be marked for extinction. Recent research at the University of

California in Los Angeles shows that our brains become very unco-
operative when we try to change behaviors and thought patterns
that have become comfortable, especially over long periods of time.
The region of our brain called the basal ganglia is responsible.
Simply speaking, it is our internal "hard drive," where we store the
behaviors we repeat, over and over again. The purpose of storing
such processes is so that we don't have to think about each of the
steps every time we do them.

Think of driving a car. Few of us think about the steps we take
to operate our cars, especially when we're in home territory. But
put yourself behind the wheel of a rental car in a city or country
you don't know in rush hour traffic, and observe what happens.
Most of us will become exhausted, quickly, and might also experience frustration, panic, hyperalertness, anxiety, and a variety of
other mind-boggling emotions. Why? Because just about everything new we experience, whether skills, ideas, products, or information, is sifted through the prefrontal cortex in the brain—our
"RAM" memory. This is where we temporarily hold anything new
until we *deliberately* act to move it to the basal ganglia for permanent residence—which happens through repetition. The prefrontal
cortex resists the new, causing us to feel uncomfortable when we
try to establish new behaviors.

To continue the rental car metaphor, consider the fact that, in
London, these autos are returned to rental companies early by a large
number of Americans visiting that city for the first time. And no
wonder. As an American driving in London, you're forced to navigate
from the "wrong side" of the road, while sitting in the "wrong seat"
in the car—at the same time that the road signs point you in con-
fusing directions. It takes only about 20 minutes before your RAM
memory is full, and begging you to return to what you know how to
do, and of course, that won't work, so we're more likely to give up.

The prefrontal cortex consumes a lot of energy in the form of
glucose, and it takes enormous effort to process anything through
it. The only way to get past this energy-intensive gate in our brain is
to "mark" the new information, skill, or idea for growth. Otherwise,

the prefrontal cortex labels it for extinction and boots it out, in favor of what we already know how to do. In contrast, the routine behavior stored in the basal ganglia is bossy, and wins a lot of arguments, unless you purposely override it. Many people prefer not to argue with their internal selves and give up just for the relief of feeling comfortable again. That's how the basal ganglia talk you into doing what you've always done. And that's why there are so many average performers out there, in comparison to successful Shortcuts.

YOU HAVE TO WANT IT

Human beings mark behaviors for growth by doing a few things very consistently. Your basal ganglia will not let just anything get into its privileged palace. You will have to reiterate, over and over again, that you really want to develop and become fluent in the new behavior. Think of your basal ganglia as muscles that you strengthen with consistent desire and activity. The only way to attain more and better skills is to first perfect one skill; and then add another skill to work on. You do this over and over again, and keep doing it until you have established enough patterned behaviors in a skill set to perform at high levels. Those who keep doing it become the pros. Those who give up get to watch the pros.

Another aspect of this process is that it forces you to choose the skills you sincerely want to develop, so as not to waste space with things that will just get in the way of you demonstrating your expertise and ability. Basketball superstar Michael Jordan is considered by many to be the greatest athlete in history. At the height of his playing career his basal ganglia required him to consistently commit to specific skills that maintained his extraordinary basketball capabilities. He stayed focused. He didn't dilute his athletic prowess to become a scratch golfer or a Wimbledon-caliber tennis player. He might have had the athletic ability to do so, but he channeled his desire and focus into what was required to achieve and maintain his quick moves, "natural" thinking, and ability on the basketball court. Few people are ever all-around brilliant at everything they try.

BE WILLING TO DO IT TODAY, TOMORROW, AND THE NEXT DAY, AND . . .

As you might guess, the first step toward achieving excellence in any field is having the desire or motivation. You must really want whatever behavior or skill you're trying to acquire. As just stated, your basal ganglia will make finding permanent storage for any new behavior very difficult, so a half-effort will fail almost every time.

Train Your Brain for 21 Days

Begin with desire, then select a focused goal that you can practice or address every single day for 21 days. On the twenty-second day, you have the *right* to continue. Note I said "right," not "habit." That's because the neural pathways that create the automatic storage and retrieval system of the basal ganglia are like fiber-optic cables. They contain several neural strands. After completing the habit-forming steps described here, the brain literally grows a new neural strand. If you cannot do something every day for 21 days, chances are you won't have a strong enough strand to lead to the firm establishment of your desired behavior. And if you give up before the 21 days, you will have to start all over again. During this 21-day period you will learn how serious you really are about acquiring a new behavior or skill.

Remember, the brain learns and stores behaviors through repetition. The basic model is:

1. See, hear about, witness and/or visualize the accomplishment of a skill.

2. Try (practice) the skill.

Train Your Brain for 21 Days (Continued)

3. Think about how the skill worked for you.

4. Adjust to improve the skill.

5. Repeat.

6. Do it every day for 21 days.

A simple way to remember the formula is as the acronym STTAR: see, try, think, adjust, and repeat. The more often you repeat the behavior, the more your brain will reward you by thickening the pathway that leads your performance of the behavior more easily and comfortably.

Keep Going—That's What the Pros Do

If you make it to 21 days, you're ready to start playing with the semipros. It takes 60 to 90 days of doing the same thing every day for the behavior to become second nature. You may still have to think about initiating it for a few seconds, but your thought process to get you there will become more rapid and increasingly comfortable.

It's only after you reach 120 to 180 days of consistent practice that you will have built a neural pathway that is stored in the basal ganglia for easy and instant retrieval. Once you establish a number of those neural pathways around a certain area of expertise, you can pretty much write your own ticket to success. If you want to shorten the time to get the behavior, you have to be willing to practice the behavior more frequently.

The next step is to visualize a realistic goal that your brain can accommodate. If, say, you want to lose 50 pounds, your brain will have a hard time imagining you 50 pounds lighter tomorrow. If, however, you say you want to lose 50 pounds beginning tomorrow with the first 10 ounces, you will more easily be able to figure out many things to get you there: say no to cream in your coffee; resist the soda at lunch, skip bread at dinner, walk briskly an extra 15 minutes after work, and so on. Your brain acknowledges those efforts and so your chances of success go up.

The basal ganglia respond to repetition. The more you consistently *do* something, the more rapidly it will become stored and depart from that energy-depleting space of the prefrontal cortex.

PUTTING THOUGHTS INTO ACTION

Let's say your desire—remember, that's step one—is to become more assertive. You want to be able to express your ideas in situations that typically make you uncomfortable—for example, with high-level executives in your organization. During the first 21 days, you might assign yourself the task of speaking up at least once every day in any situation where you might have previously stayed quiet. Even if it's scary, and even if your basal ganglia and prefrontal cortex are arguing and making you feel uncomfortable, you still speak up. You might say: "I have a thought about that. May I share it?"

After 21 days, speaking up will feel easier. It probably will continue to be somewhat anxiety-provoking, but you'll have gained some confidence. Continue to make the conscious choice to speak up until you hit the 90-day mark. Notice along the way how you feel and how people respond. You might find that you are now asked your opinion on a regular basis; and you might also discover that you've become more deeply involved in all aspects of your work. Probably, the feedback from others will be positive, overall, although there will always be some people who resist change, no matter where or who it comes from. As long as it's working for you, keep going. One good way to track your improvement is to note your observations in a journal. But however you manage to do it, keep on going.

When you've been using the new behavior consistently for approximately 120 to 180 days, it will be a part of you, at a level most don't achieve. That's because you kept going.

Many people make progress more quickly when they have someone holding them accountable or cheering them—coaches, advisors, or supporters of any stripe. To heighten and speed your learning process, ask for help—and then listen to what they say.

WORKING OUT LIKE A SHORTCUT

Once you've added one behavior or skill to your repertoire, you're ready for another new success behavior. As you proceed, you'll find that the more adept you become at learning, the more layers you will be able to add simultaneously. The brain is like a muscle, and the more you exercise it, the more you can do with it—the more you learn, the more you *can* learn.

Keep in mind, it's a dog-eat-dog world out there, and if you're not willing to become a Shortcut, there is always someone else who is. To survive, you have to be willing to—at your own expense, if necessary—upgrade your skills and knowledge constantly. All too often people are hired and they are effective Shortcuts for a while, but then they are asked to do more. Perhaps they complain that their organization does not "provide" the training they need. Here's the hard reality: it's not your organization's job to turn you into a marketable commodity. Good companies certainly try to provide what is necessary to help their employees succeed; but it's next to impossible for them to meet everyone's needs—nor should they be expected to do so. Many companies do, however, offer workshops, and even college tuition reimbursement programs. Interestingly, however, according to data from the American Society of Training and Development, only a small percentage of employees use their companies' college tuition reimbursement offerings. My point is, the competition to become a successful Shortcut is not as stiff as you might think. So just go out there and do it! No one should be more interested in your success than you are; if you wait for someone else to achieve it for you, you'll be waiting a long time.

Life is one ongoing lesson, and throughout yours you'll be given a plethora of opportunities to make you smarter and more valuable. It's up to you, and no one else, to take advantage of those opportunities, to take responsibility for making yourself more valuable.

To become a Shortcut superstar, you have to go through the struggle, and focus on that first behavioral/skill addition or change. You, too, can beat the odds, if you keep on going.

Shortcut Lesson

Your skills, both professional and personal, will undoubtedly need to be "upgraded" along the way if you are to remain competitive and at your best. The system described here can make that happen for you. Yes, it takes time, dedication, and desire. The reward is great, however, and, you'll be among the few who can consider themselves superstar Shortcuts.

Incite Your Insights

All of the top achievers I know are life-long learners . . .
looking for new skills, insights, and ideas. If they're not
learning, they're not growing . . . not moving toward
excellence.

—Dennis Waitley
speaker and author

Do you ever wonder when it will be your turn? Your turn for the
big job? Your turn to be the person others look to, and rely upon?

You get to be that person when you hone "the big gun"
Shortcut—insight. Insight is the ultimate Shortcut: it is the differ-
entiator that defines careers every day. The insightful person is a
much-praised and coveted Shortcut because he or she offers that
quick assessment, uncanny observation, or revolutionary thought
that brings corporations billions of dollars in revenue or cost con-
tainment. It's the stuff of experience and courage, the kind you get
when you work through mastery; and the more you work to master
something, the more insight and confidence you acquire. It's our
experience, not our *years* of experience on the job, that translates to
the powerhouse we call insight. It's a nice little circle of life.

There is good news and bad news here. The good news is that
insight is yours if you pay attention to the right things. The bad
news is that without effort on your part, achieving insight probably won't happen. The process fits in with mastery, and it takes
dedication and practice and courage. You will be pleased to know,
however, that you already have what it takes to get started: your
personal experiences. These, combined with the information that is
readily available to you, can make all of the difference in the world.

The reality is that I can know what you know, and you
can know what I know. We all have access to most of the same

information as the next person. The Internet makes that possible. Today, billions of pages of information are available to anyone, anywhere, anytime. What does this all mean? That the lines are increasingly becoming blurred between the good and the great.

It used to be that those who were great were the ones with the most information or knowledge. But now widespread access to all kinds of information in all fields is only keystrokes away for everyone. Historically, the intellectually superior were the rulers of the business world. Not so any longer. Daniel Pink submits in his brilliant book *A Whole New Mind*[14] that when facts become so easy to obtain by anyone, anywhere, anytime, those facts lose their glamour and value. We've all experienced having a juicy piece of news that we can't wait to tell a friend or colleague. We're excited because we're the "owner" of the morsel; and with great drama, we share the information, only to find out our friend already knew it. Talk about taking the wind out of your sails!

But that's just the way it is. Information no longer has the impact it once did; instead, the power now lies in how it is applied to make our lives easier or better. And so the leaders of the foreseeable future are those with insight. Albert Einstein recognized this decades ago. He refused to memorize anything that he could readily find in a book, thus leaving space in his brain for him to think and create. Einstein is known not for his ability to memorize and remember vast amounts of information, but for his ability to create and provide insight.

So, if information or data alone isn't enough to make us successful, then what does it take? The answer is this: It's the life we give to the data that separates the good from the great. It's the insight we glean from the data—easy as that.

But wait a minute; not so easy. What is insight, and where does it come from?

Insight is the reframing of old or current news into something innovative and useable for the future. It's the product that results from the *meeting* between data and experience. Your competitive edge—your insight—is distinguished because you and your life experiences are unique. They are something about you that no one else shares.

Consider a product named as one of the best inventions of 2005. It was recognized and subsequently adopted by Target stores as a valuable Shortcut, and it was the result of insight. It's a prescription drug bottle, conceived by graphic designer Deborah Adler, an idea that turned bottle design upside down—literally. The bottle stands on its cap. It is flat, not round, making it possible to read the labels without turning the bottle. Why is this so revolutionary? Today, millions of baby boomers are taking more and more prescription drugs, along with the growing number of people who are living well into their 70s and 80s. The flat design allows for less confusion and increased ease of handling. The bottles also come with colored rings to put around the mouth of the bottles so that different members of the family don't mix up their prescriptions. Mom gets yellow, Dad gets green, and so on. Warnings and pullout information are on the flip side of the bottle. The design is considered so innovative that a sample bottle is on display at the world-famous Modern Museum of Art in New York City.

Where did Deborah's insight come from? A meeting of her knowledge, in this case design, with one of her life experiences. As it turns out, Deborah's grandmother once mistakenly took her husband's pills instead of her own. *Bam!* A brand new Shortcut devised by a Shortcut who used the Shortcut of insight.

Where does such insight happen in the halls of the corporate universe? The executive offices in America resound with the challenge to the rank and file: "Help us make this place fabulously successful." Most growth in corporations is a mixture of merger/acquisition (M&A) activity and so-called organic growth—the kind that comes from taking something already available and turning it on its head. It certainly takes insight to pick the right companies to merge or acquire. But I want to talk about organic growth, because this is where most people can make their insight count in companies.

Let's assume (although of course it's not true across the board) that most top executives have gotten their high-level jobs because of insights they've contributed over the years. Through a combination of knowledge and their unique personal experiences, they have found ways to contribute, innovate, and excel in ways that set them apart from others in their field. This is the challenge that all aspiring leaders must try to meet, and that those who "have made it" must try to sustain. M&A scenarios are short-lived. Wall Street rewards organizations only briefly for making an excellent marriage between two companies; it's sustainable growth that matters long term. Wall Street demands and then rewards companies that consistently offer new insight. Look at Microsoft, Apple, Intel, GE, Motorola, Medtronic, Johnson & Johnson, Siemens, and other venerable, innovative companies. They hire the best insight money can buy to come up with the newest twist to their product offerings. Apple's iPhone revolutionized the cellular device industry. But just as soon as the iPhone was released, competitors were creating their own versions. It's a constant race. Who's going to be the company to come up with the next great automobile, phone, or medical device? There's a never-ending need for insight. It's bankable, and it takes a good deal of work to sustain it.

Sustained insight might be the most challenging goal of all to achieve, because once you've "made it," you can't just rest on your laurels. As we've all observed, the people who have moved up the corporate ladder based on their insights often find themselves struggling to come up with new ones. In the face of constant demands to understand and focus on data, they also are expected to continue to have insightful ideas. The tragedy is that in managing data, they too often find that they no longer have time to think and reflect—the very processes that got them where they are.

Recall the Yerkes-Dodson Law of performance and anxiety I introduced earlier. It basically says that a bit of anxious tension can give us an edge to create. But if we stay mired in that anxiety for too long, we hit a point of diminishing returns and can no longer generate new ideas (insight). Think about executives who, to the exclusion of all else, focus on preparing quarterly earnings releases for Wall Street, only to be met with the same frenzy in a few more months. When do they have time to stop and reflect? When do they have time to think about new insights? And what is the cost of this constant whirl of activity to the company and to the individuals? Insight takes nurturing and practice; it won't leap off a page of numbers in a flash of brilliance.

Today, anxiety in organizations is at an all-time high, and employees—even the most experienced—are in reactionary mode. The result is that relatively little creation is happening. The Yerkes-Dodson Law says that once maximum anxiety is reached, a break must be taken—there must be a literal walking away from the project, the numbers, the issue at hand—in order to create insight for something new.

Remember the last time you were up against a major deadline at work? You may have stayed up into the wee hours of the morning to complete it. Now, think about your process and your productivity, as you became more anxious and tired. You probably fell into old patterns to complete the project, perhaps consulting past reports, adopting a tried-and-true template, and possibly resorting to conclusions that worked once before. Did you create something new or bring new insight? Or were you just happy to have the PowerPoint deck and support materials complete and looking nice? All too often, that is the barometer of a job well done. But ask yourself, what real value did you bring? What good did you do for you or for your company? It is only when you are able to say, "I brought insight" that you will be noticed. And it is only then that you will be steps closer to taking your place "at the table."

A valuable activity that will help you to develop your insight is to dust off your past and begin to mine it for lessons. Many of the lessons will emerge as you recall difficult times, crisis points, defining moments, and even tragedy. Lessons are buried there, if you are willing to look. Another approach is to consider the parallels and similarities between seemingly different things. The trick is to expand your thinking beyond business. Think about the things you've experienced, and write them down. What did you learn? You may not have a ready application for the lessons, but when the moment appears, your awareness of your experiences will lead to insight.

Early in my television career, I won several awards for writing and producing. About 15 years ago, I went through this very exercise, of mining my past and looking for parallels. I noticed a pattern that was actually wreaking havoc with my mind and my career. When I examined my past, I noticed that every time I won a major award in television, I changed jobs. Sometimes, I changed companies altogether. The insight that came to me was that instead of working on deepening my strengths and abilities, I viewed the awards as proof that I could already "do it," and so moved on to the next thing. The same pattern began to emerge after I changed careers, to become a speaker and adult educator. I made a go of talking about customer service, team building, leadership, negotiations—you name it, I probably talked about it. I'm a quick study, and people consider me to be intuitive about human interaction—those characteristics I would put into my strength box. But at the same time I was feeling inauthentic and not very accomplished. By dusting off my past and looking at the parallels of how I behaved when I achieved something, I saw myself repeating that very thing, and it wasn't serving me well. I would talk on a topic, and instead of delving deeply into it, once I mastered the basics I moved on. I didn't stick with anything for long. That insight led to my dedication to the field of studying success behaviors. Insight moved me to the product and body of knowledge I represent now, and have for the last 15 years.

Exercise

Here are some excellent questions to ask to inspire insight:

- If our/my competitor had my product or service, what would they do with it?

- What is *my* opinion about what we're doing in our company?

- How would I go about turning things around at the company? Why would I take that route?

- How do I see a particular issue differently than others and why would it be valuable to communicate?

- What will it take for me to raise my hand and volunteer my opinion?

Shortcut Lesson

The competitive edge you have is neither the result of the data you have nor your experience alone, but both combined, and seasoned with reflection. They give you something no other living person on the planet has: your distinctive insight. Trust yourself. Practice insight. Practice verbalizing it to others. Practice allowing others to improve upon it. Practice pushing the elevator to the top floor. That's where your seat is awaiting you, at the table.

Throw Some Spice on the Grill

How to Stand Out with Just a Little Bit of Creativity

> Creativity is the natural extension of our enthusiasm.
> —EARL NIGHTINGALE
> *author*

A group of top chefs was competing for big money and fame on the Food Network. One of their assignments was given by heavy-hitter food magazine *Bon Appetit*. The winner would have his or her culinary creation featured in a special issue of the magazine—an enormous resume booster.

The mission from *Bon Appetit* was simple: create a meal that average home cooks could easily reproduce on their backyard grill. Chef after chef presented their recipes to the editors of the magazine and the celebrity judges. There was rack of lamb, chicken à la something-hard-to-pronounce, cedar-planked fish, a big hunk of beef, and plain old grilled chicken. As the judges talked candidly about each of the backyard fare presentations, they repeatedly said they couldn't imagine the average person using most of the recipes . . . except—you guessed it—the chef who made the plain old chicken.

His recipe wasn't fancy; he told the judges that his secret was to take a big handful of his very favorite spices and literally throw them on the grill while the chicken was cooking. The resultant flavor pleased palates from the most simple to sophisticated, and the judges loved this. Thus, this competitor had followed the instructions: to create something most of us would try, but he also added a very simple Shortcut to make an otherwise bland and ordinary meal special. Ultimately, he did not win first place in the competition; but he did take second place, not bad for plain old grilled chicken.

Shortcut Lesson

Shortcuts are so good at what they do that they have the time to be more creative and add spice to their skill, whatever it is. And they look forward to it. They know they don't necessarily have to have the next big idea; but thanks to their mastery, they can visualize and utilize the little things that make a big difference in even the simplest thing.

Use the White Space

Silence within silence, no words within blank space,
nothing on blank page, less within the void.

—JALAL AD-DIN RUMI
thirteenth century Persian mystic and poet

You may have seen this Gestalt-type drawing, from which you're supposed to guess the age of the woman in it. Such exercises can be frustrating, even if you've done them several times. Some people see a very young woman; others see a very old woman; still others can distinguish both. Being able to see both requires adjusting the way you look at the drawing, particularly if you've never looked at such a picture before. But after a bit of practice, you start to adjust your vision, enabling you to see what is really there—even if initially you can't.

Shortcuts are good at seeing what might be missing, and then filling it in. They notice something in the white space around the image, not just the image itself. In other words, they look beyond the obvious to find answers. That skill makes all the difference between a Shortcut and the average person. With that in mind, take a look at the drawing made famous by psychologist Edgar Rubin, in 1915. A Shortcut would see both the vase and the two human profiles, as well.

A few years ago, a corporate finance officer of a large, multi-billion-dollar corporation was describing to me why she wanted her direct reports to increase their critical thinking abilities. She explained this in a most interesting way: "When I ask people for a report or a set of numbers, they bring me what I want. But, they don't necessarily bring me what I *need*." She went on to say that the brain power in her organization was tremendous, but that everyone was so busy in their individual realms that they didn't have time to do anything but respond to specific requests. Thus, there was a lack of *conceptual thought*. Therefore, she added, she's always pleasantly surprised when someone does takes the time to listen to her request, ask a few questions, bring her what she asked for, along with what they believe she was actually requesting. She says that such a person is worth his or her weight in gold, and that she would love to surround herself with thinkers like this—that is, she wants Shortcuts who are immersed enough in the subject matter to see the bigger picture and respond beyond the obvious request.

Exercise

Create white space thinking by examining projects and issues with a critical eye. Ask:

- What is missing?

- What else can be deduced from this data/project/issue?

- How would a non-expert on this material view it?

- Boiled down to simplicity, what is really being communicated here?

- What is really being requested?

- What doesn't the requestor know that I do that could enhance this data/project/issue?

Shortcut Lesson

Shortcuts ask enough questions to help them see the white space, and they are rewarded for it accordingly. When they deliver, they give not only what is requested but anything else that might be needed, as well. When you're an expert, you're more able to see the white space because you have broader experiences.

Excel as a White Belt First

Sometimes you do what you have to do in order to do what you want to do.

—Anonymous

My first professional job was as an associate news producer at a television station in Denver. Back then, an associate producer was a euphemism for a gopher; the job was all title and very little pay. Patti Dennis, the producer I worked with, was one of the best and most honest mentors I've had in my life. I continue to hear her voice in my head to this day

After being on the job for about four months, I began to get bored; I wanted to be a full producer. One day when I was feeling particularly frustrated and undervalued, I asked Patti, a little pointedly, "When am I going to be able to be a producer?" I explained that I had learned everything I could about being an associate producer, and that it was time to move on. With her laserlike honesty, she stopped typing, looked directly in my eyes and said, "Scott, the only way you'll become a full producer is to become the best associate producer any of us have seen. You're good at what you do, but not so good yet that it makes up for all the complaining you do about it."

She went back to work while I considered the life lesson she had just taught me. I took to heart what she said, and put my head down and went about my work with as much intensity and determination as I could muster. I stopped worrying about what I wanted to grow up to be; instead I focused on what I was. And Patti was right. Three months after my conversation with her, the upper news management noticed my efforts, and I was rewarded with a producer position.

I learned a similar lesson when I was taking a martial arts class. The sensei (teacher) would regularly require the black belt students to give up their black belts for three months and behave again as white belts. At first, I thought this was just a little control ploy to teach the black belts who was boss. It wasn't. It was a part of the process to become a master. It was a reminder that wherever you are, that is where you should be. The best Shortcuts get that way because they know that everything along the path toward mastery is a lesson that will serve them today and in the future. They understand that being a white belt is necessary to become a black belt. No one starts as a black belt. They first became proficient at the basics so that they can excel at the highest levels.

One woman I particularly admire in this regard is Tina. She's a contact for our company whose job it is to attend to the incredible amount of detail that needs to be addressed before I show up for a program at her company. One morning before class, she met me very early—6:30 A.M.—at the front desk so that I could be prepared when the participants walked in an hour later. As I set up, I chatted with Tina about her job and how appreciative I was of all she did to make things go so smoothly on her end. She thanked me; then we continued to talk, specifically, I asked about her aspirations at the company. She said, "I plan to get so good at what I'm doing now that my boss will have no choice but to let me do what I'm really good at—*big* meeting planning."

How refreshing, I thought. Here's someone performing a job that many meeting planners would feel is beneath them. But Tina took it as her challenge to make the job a stepping stone; and the first step was to prove that she excelled at planning smaller meetings. This was all the more impressive when I subsequently learned that Tina had previously owned her own meeting planning firm before being hired in-house at her current company. So, in fact, her skills already extended beyond the scope of the role she was now filling. Yet what I experienced with Tina was not impatience or frustration, but someone who prided herself in performing well at any level, someone with an incredible energy and attitude—even at 6:30 in the morning!—and someone who treated no detail as too small to warrant her full attention.

When Tina feels like she's mastered her job, and the attendant organizational politics, she says she'll be ready to ask for the upper-level position; and my bet is the company will bend over backward to create something for her, if there's no position open already.

Shortcut Lesson

Shortcuts become the best at what they do on their way to becoming something better.

Get Framed

Art consists of limitation. The most beautiful part of
every picture is the frame.

—G. K. CHESTERTON
nineteenth– to twentieth-century critic and novelist

When I was paring down my possessions in preparation for
a move to a new house, I found myself ruthlessly tossing
away mementos and other items I hadn't looked at or used since the last
move. In a basement storage closet, I came upon an oil painting I had
bought on eBay. It was a drab-looking $20 painting of trees—
I couldn't recall why I had purchased it in the first place. Somehow,
however, the painting made it to my new home. I decided that if it
had the cosmic capability to stay with me, I should resurrect it and
give it a new life. And so I reframed it.

When that picture came back from the frame shop, I was
astounded at the difference. I hung it where everyone could see it,
and marveled how many people commented on how much they
liked it. More than a few also hinted that I must have spent a lot of
money on it. The truth is, the frame cost several times more than
the painting, but it made all the difference in the world—turning a
$20 painting into a minor masterpiece.

Framing, or reframing, is one of the single most important
things we can do to jump-start and rekindle professional relationships. Not only is it essential to communicating our ideas, it's a
Shortcut's greatest tool for getting to the heart of a matter quickly
and effectively. It demonstrates the Shortcut principle of: "I'm good
enough at what I do that I can frame my work in myriad different
ways so that people can understand it, no matter what their experience with my area."

Too many of us tend to think that if our information is solid, it alone should be enough to get the job done. That is framing that doesn't serve us very well in most cases. Several years ago, while coaching an executive about powerful presentations, I had one of those moments of clarity that sometimes comes after doing something over and over. The executive was struggling with the concept of radically rearranging his data for various audiences. He argued that because those who listen to his presentations are smart businesspeople, they should all be at the same level of understanding; otherwise, they shouldn't be in their jobs.

That's a narrow view of people, I told him, one that won't get many to see his way of thinking. But I couldn't get through to him. So, in exasperation, I attempted to reframe this crucial point for him. I asked him first to present one aspect of his presentation to me as if I were a high school student. He did a great job of "dumbing down" the material. Next I asked him to do the same thing, pretending I was a neighbor of his in a different line of business; then a colleague in a different department; next, an associate with a different background; and, finally, a coworker with a different opinion from his. He got my point, which, ironically, was the point of my efforts: to help him share his information effectively, and to become a Shortcut to understanding. It changed the way he presented and communicated overall. Over the subsequent months, the response from his audiences was overwhelmingly positive. All he had to do was reframe the same material, making it a Shortcut to understanding for different people. He no longer believes that his job is to impress people with his knowledge but, rather, to allow people to be impressed with themselves by understanding the information he is presenting.

Shortcuts take the time and energy to consider carefully how to say or do something so that people of various backgrounds and training can get equal value from their information and expertise. They focus as closely on how they "frame" their information as on the content itself. They know that their expertise won't be understood the same way by Jane as it is by John, and so they wisely take into account the differences among people.

Shortcut Lesson

When all is said and done, the Shortcut is the person who uses the right mix of words and actions to reach his or her audience. An effective Shortcut knows that he or she might need to reframe their presentations to make them stand out and be noticed. Shortcuts are so good at what they do that they have the ability to adjust as required to suit their audience.

Be the Influencer

> Every sale has five basic obstacles: no need, no money,
> no hurry, no desire, no trust.
>
> —Zig Ziglar
> *speaker and author*

Influence. Most of us want more of it. At the same time, we're often hard-pressed to explain just what influence is, and why we feel such a need to wield it. And that's what makes "influence" a million-dollar word. It's a Shortcut in and of itself.

Somewhere along the way, "influence" earned a respectable reputation, and people seem to associate it with positive and powerful characteristics. It is only by understanding what influence really is, however, that you can see why it is so . . . well . . . influential. From that, you can learn how to increase your influence as a Shortcut.

There are many definitions of influence, and volumes have been written about it. My intention here is not to rehash what's already been covered, but to recast influence as something I truly believe anyone, at any level, can have. In my view, influence isn't only for powerful people bearing impressive titles, commanding enormous salaries. Influence can be used in all areas of life, with your children and friends and colleagues and clients.

Influence also is not, in my opinion, about getting something you want in any particular instance, simply because you were able to, for example, use the right combination of words at the right time. No, from my point of view, influence can be defined with one five-letter word: "trust."

Moreover, I want to make the distinction between *influence* and *persuasion*. Though both are useful and necessary, most people in my workshops who ask me how to become an influential Shortcut confuse the two terms and the benefits each brings. Here is the simple, Shortcut way to look at it: *Influence is what you get when you take the time to build trust.* It's the result of a series of events over time between two parties. To have influence, and to turn it into a Shortcut, you have to spend the time. Rarely can you have true, long-term influence without spending the time to nurture the trust that is required to earn it. Once you have built this connection, you become influential; you can pick up the phone and, without a lot of fanfare, set the wheels in motion to get you what you need or want.

Put this in the context of a business relationship with someone you've known and trusted for a long time. When your trust level is high for a person, you don't spend a lot of time on due diligence. You are influenced by the person because you have faith in his or her advice. It is reliable. It is something you have experienced time and again. It fits the formula for trust, consistent behavior over a period of time. And when someone asks you who you know to take care of a similar issue, without hesitation you recommend that influential person. On and on the circle of influence grows. The more people you have in your pipeline with whom you've established that level of trust, the more influence you have. It is simple, and true.

Persuasion, in contrast, is required when trust is low. Do not confuse a lack of trust with bad feelings or dishonesty, though. The need for trust can occur between two people simply because they don't know each other. Well-researched and thought-out data is required when you're in a persuasive mode. Since you don't yet have a relationship built on trust, the decision has to be predicated on something—in this case, the facts. The problem with persuasion is that data can be interpreted in many ways; so when you do not yet have influence, your argument can fall apart very quickly. For example, you'll need to be persuasive when you make that first presentation to your company's bigwigs. They don't know you, so your data will have to be extremely well developed and thorough. Over time, however, as you present more often to these execs, and they come to rely on you, you will become more influential;

eventually, you will need to do little more than show up and present your case, simply and without a lot of fanfare. That's persuasion turned into influence, and it is powerful.

How do you become influential? First, have patience. I know an executive—let's call him Bill—who took a high-level corporate job. He came in with his own agenda, and within 30 days of his start date had made sweeping changes. But although he had the authority to make people do what he wanted, he lacked the relationship-building skills necessary to become influential; the more immediate result among his direct reports was animosity and low morale. Over time, employees began to leave the company in droves. Still, Bill continued to wield his authority to get people to perform. But because he had no lasting influence he became increasingly frustrated. Even high-ranking employees questioned his strategies and motives. Eventually, Bill became so ineffective that the company's board finally asked him to step down.

The major ingredient missing from Bill's leadership style was trust. As noted, trust takes time to build. It is not a "soft" skill, a luxury; it is a requirement for success. Take a look at the most powerful and admired executives you know, and my bet is they have built trust, and through that, influence.

You build influence one relationship at a time. You do it by listening to people, by actually getting to know people and what's going on in both their personal and professional worlds. Recognition is another great trust builder that leads to influence. When you recognize the excellent work of others, especially publicly, they will begin to feel safe around you. Eventually, they will see you are looking out for their best interests, as well; so when you ask them to do something, they will not require all the data of persuasion. They will trust you and, thus, perform. That is influence in action.

Both persuasion and influence came into play during an important part of my life. The first few years after I left television, I continued to freelance. During this period, a colleague recommended me to the local Arthritis Foundation to do a television telethon for them—similar to the Jerry Lewis muscular dystrophy telethon. I had experience with that kind of format, so when I met with the board of the foundation, I used all of my powers of persuasion to convince them *not* to do a telethon. I told them, it's a lot of work, costs big dollars, and the payoff isn't significant unless you have a name like a Jerry Lewis behind it. We talked and talked, and I tried to persuade. I presented dollar figures to show the enormous expenses and relative low return associated with the format. At the same time, I proposed an alternative approach for their consideration. After about three weeks of back and forth negotiations, and still no decision on their part, I told them that if they decided to do a telethon, I wasn't their man.

Finally, they reluctantly made a decision, choosing to go with the alternative programming I had recommended. I convinced them, through lots of charts and numbers and presentations, to allow me to write and produce a week-long campaign, which we called "Haven't Got Time for the Pain." It was a multitiered effort, involving TV, newspaper, radio, corporate challenges, a mail-stuffer in energy company bills in Colorado (over a million), and airline and other prize giveaways. We also lined up doctors to serve on an arthritis hotline from the National Jewish Hospital, world renowned for its work in rheumatology. It was going to be a big deal, I promised. The looks on the board members' faces said it all: "We'll see. You'd better not mess this up."

The selling point for all of the different stakeholders was the television aspect—they all wanted the mega-reach that TV promised. The problem was, I hadn't approached anyone in television yet; I had only proposed it as part of the mix. I was betting on my relationships in television to make it happen.

I contacted the news director at KCNC-TV in Denver, and he agreed to let me stop in to run my idea by him. Fifteen minutes into our discussion—five minutes of which was spent with "what's up with you?" chit-chat—I had a deal for twice-daily prime-time news reports on arthritis for a week; a helpline set up by the station for the doctors to answer calls; and a three-times daily, 30-second promotional announcement of the corporate winners in the challenge. This was no small feat. I hadn't given much data to the news director; only concepts and the fact that arthritis is nearly disabling for at least a quarter of the population. The deciding factor for him was the fact that he knew my work; he trusted it. He knew that if I was pitching for it, I had done my homework and it would most likely fit for the station. But it took 10 years of toil in television to get to the point where I could have that kind of influence in 15 minutes.

I'm proud to report that the campaign went on to raise thousands of dollars for the Arthritis Foundation, and brought great awareness to millions of viewers. Hundreds called in each day for a week to the physician hotline. Ultimately, the campaign won a prestigious award from the National Arthritis Foundation for the television category; *People* magazine and the *Washington Post* were the magazine and newspaper award winners, respectively.

It is clear that, initially, this scenario had posed a lot of risk for many people. During the first phase, I had to use persuasion, because I had no relationship with the people at the foundation. It took several weeks to convince them, and they were still uncertain until the entire proposal was complete. Persuasion requires a lot of data and well-constructed arguments.

During the television negotiation phase, it was different, because I had already built trust in that arena. The news director knew my work, and so within a few minutes, a major deal was cut. That is the power of influence. How do you get it? Again, by building one trusting relationship at a time and proving that you are good to your word. To begin, you'll need to use persuasion—data and sound arguments—but over time, and with patience, you gain influence. In sum, there is no Shortcut for influence. It takes time and patience. Influence is a Shortcut only after you have achieved it.

My business partner, Marty Lassen, is another example of an influential Shortcut. She has deposited many hours into the credibility and trust bank with many people. Recently she was asked by a trusted business friend, Barb, to make an introduction to a big-name executive. Marty called the executive and asked her to take Barb's call, telling her that she trusted Barb. That's all it took. Marty's influence connected Barb with the executive. Without it, the executive would not have taken Barb's call. Influence at its best is mutually beneficial. And when trust is high, not a lot of time is spent doing due diligence—the diligence was done a long time ago. It's a Shortcut.

Another easy way to attain influence is to make yourself known; make others comfortable with you. This happens through seemingly small acts, such as taking the person you're trying to influence to coffee, taking a walk with them around the company campus, or simply talking to them without an agenda. These actions are deposits in the trust bank, which lead to influence.

Here's an example. Anthony, one of our clients working with Marty, was planning to request money for a project from the finance people in his company. In the process, Marty was surprised to learn that even though Anthony was about to ask for millions of dollars, he had formed absolutely no relationships with the people who would be considering his request. More surprising, Anthony told her, these people worked in the same location as he, yet he had never made the effort to meet them.

Marty asked Anthony, "Why not go meet them before you find yourself in the room with them for the first time, when they are predisposed to say no?" Anthony was taken aback by the simple brilliance of this idea. He agreed to engage in this small "influence event"; he was going to take a small amount of time to make these strangers familiar and comfortable with him before asking them for something.

The point of this story is that influence is a right you have to earn—you have to invest in the trust bank before you can spend influence. And it's not just the big investments that add up; you can earn influence through small deeds, too. Influence, after all, is almost always gained over a period of time.

I want to make one more important point here, about the fragility of influence. Banking giant Bear Stearns lost billions of dollars in market value, with its stock dropping from $70.00 per share to just over $2.00 per share in a matter of days. Although Bear Stearns historically has been one of the most venerable investment banking firms in the world, its largest clients lost trust and ran with their money. It took 85 years for Bear Stearns to build its influence and just four days to lose it. When you have done the work to gain trust, don't forget the responsibility that comes with it: you have to deliver. If you don't, you will lose that trust very quickly.

Exercise

1. Write down the name of someone you would like to influence.

2. Ask yourself what you can do to make his or her life easier (do something easy for you but not so for him or her).

3. Do something to make his or her life better (introduce the person to someone who represents revenue or a solution to a problem, for example).

4. Determine how you will get in front of this person, to "perform."

5. If you don't know this person, ask who you *do* know who has this person's trust and is willing to introduce you.

6. If you already know this person, decide how you are going to nurture your connection with him or her (doing a favor, taking him/her to coffee or lunch, offering information that is interesting and valuable).

Shortcut Lesson

The most successful Shortcuts are influential. They are consistent, garnering deep trust from many people. In the end, it's the trust you earn through dependable delivery that makes you influential. You have to work at it. Influence is not a birthright.

PART THREE

The Know-How

> Basically, likeability comes down to creating positive emotional experiences in others. . . . When you make others feel good, they tend to gravitate to you.
>
> —TIM SANDERS
> *author,* The Likeability Factor

LIKEABILITY: THE QUICKEST PERSONAL SHORTCUT

There are few things that will help you in your life and your job as much as likeability. Being likeable is one of the most influential things you will ever be; and we're all just big kids at heart when it comes to wanting to be liked.

Take a look at any school-aged child on a playground, and you'll see the power of likeability at work. Kids tend to gravitate to other kids who act like them, dress like them, and think and talk like them; they are attracted to others who think they're cool, funny, and cute. Children begin the struggle to gain the upper hand early on by tallying the number of people who like them—a battle for the "power of the playground." That doesn't change as we grow into adults; the playground just looks different. Likeability is the grease that keeps both personal and professional relationships running smoothly; and our desire to attain it begins in preschool.

We make lifelong decisions based on the powerful elixir of likeability; and none of us is exempt from its influence. Dr. Robert Cialdini, author of *The Influence: Science and Practice,* and others have studied the power of likeability, and concluded that it is one of the most potent of influencers in our day-to-day decision making.

My own experiences have proven this true time and again. For example, I recall being in line to check in to a hotel, along with hundreds of people, all of whom were arriving to attend various conventions. It was a flurry of activity, and I noticed the man ahead of me was becoming visibly agitated.

"What do you mean you don't have a room for me?!," he shouted. Handing a piece of paper to the clerk, he demanded, "What do you call this? I call it a confirmation! Get me a room or get me the manager!" The rest of us began to look at each other uncomfortably, in particular feeling embarrassed on behalf of the clerk he was berating. She explained to him that, unfortunately, the hotel had oversold, but that she would gladly book him into any one of three other nearby hotels and have him shuttled over. He would have none of it, and again demanded to talk to the manager.

When the manager appeared on the scene, this man again launched into his "I'm-the-customer-and-an-important-one" routine. At this point, it was becoming comical. The hotel manager took the man aside to deal with him, making way for me to approach the counter.

I said to the clerk, "I heard you say the Marriott was a choice. I'll go there if it's still available. And, by the way, I'm embarrassed if that man is here with the same conference I am. You should make him sleep in the parking lot."

The clerk softened a bit, smiled sardonically, and said, "Well, one of the things that happens around this time of day is that people cancel, and we've just had one. It's a junior suite, and it looks like it now has your name on it. Thank you for being civil."

Knock me over with a feather. I got to stay in one of those rooms most of us only get to see in the marketing brochure; more, I was charged the same price as a regular room.

That experience, and the lesson it taught me, remains with me to this day because it is representative of a universal truth that we know but forget sometimes: Behaving in a nasty way doesn't get us anything. It might feel good for a few seconds, as we blow off steam and put someone "in their place"; but it doesn't elicit the results we want. We're not likeable in those moments, and when it's between nasty and likeable, the victory will always go to the likeable.

Business deals begin with likeability; it is a significant factor in deciding who gets promoted and who doesn't. It is a factor in the hiring process, albeit often a subconscious one; and it inevitably sways decision makers working on multibillion-dollar transactions.

On the personal side, likeability leads us to the friends we make and keep throughout our lifetime. It can turn into love and/or partnering. Suffice it to say, likeability colors and affects most key aspects of our life.

What constitutes likeability? Probably it's different for each of us, but most people, including social scientists, would agree on a number of common attributes. These traits are:

- *Physical attractiveness.* There's no use denying it, we are initially attracted to others by their physical features—height, weight, skin color, hair style, facial features, and clothing. Of course, what is physically attractive is different for each of us; at the same time, beauty and health magazines consistently attempt to set standards of what is considered to be physically appealing. Interestingly, many buy into it, spending billions of dollars every year to perfect their faces, tone their bodies, coif their hair, and drape themselves in stylish clothes. But as the saying goes, beauty is only skin deep. Most of us can recall meeting a physically attractive person only to be repelled the moment that he or she opened his or her mouth. If a person's intellect, morals, or sense of humor aren't up to our standards, a person's physical attractiveness can be "trumped" by more compelling and meaningful attributes of likeability.

- *Similarity.* Similarity is probably the most dominant factor of likeability. It is the "me-too" factor, and it is another reason that physical attractiveness can work against someone. We're drawn to those who are like us; they make us comfortable more readily. In the movie *Shrek*, the not-so-attractive leading man gets the beautiful princess, and their relationship lasts because they have much in common. Certainly, we enjoy people who are different from us, too; but most relationships that last do so because of shared or similar interests. Too much dissimilarity creates a chasm that becomes difficult to bridge over time. That is one reason likeable people make a conscious effort to help those around them feel comfortable by focusing on those things they have in common. Sometimes, this takes extra effort, but likeable people are willing to put it in. They ask a lot of questions about the other person, and when they discover a commonality, they explore it more deeply.

- *Recognition and Complimenting.* The ability to recognize the efforts or achievements of another person, and to give a sincere compliment, is another important likeability factor. When someone acknowledges our efforts, whether for our work, the way we dress or keep house, or garden—anything we take pride in—we are drawn to them. The old saying is that flattery will get you nowhere; but, in fact, flattery will get you somewhere, especially when it is sincere. Take the time to recognize people's efforts, whether on the job or at home, and watch the magic of likeability at work.

- *Cooperation.* Let's face it; it's simply easier to like people we get along with. Common sense, I know, but it deserves mention. And this is not to say that you have to agree with people all the time. It is to say that you will experience greater success with people when you look for common ground, while respecting the differences in opinion that inevitably arise and finding a way to cooperate in spite of them.

These four likeability factors may seem apparent on paper; yet in practice they're not so simple. We can all be more likeable; it just takes awareness and consistency. Give it a try. Pay a genuine compliment. Ask some questions that will help you to discover similarities in another person. Remember a coworker's birthday. You might be surprised at the return on your "investment"; moreover, you'll appreciate how much easier your own life becomes, when others reach out to return the favor when you need it most.

I still have the birthday card my business partner Marty Lassen gave to me several years ago. I first read it at a party while I was opening other gifts and cards, so I didn't really focus on it at the time. But later, when all my friends were gone and it was quiet in my house, I read through all the cards again. Marty's read: "You are not only witty in yourself, but the cause that is wit in other people. You make me make myself laugh." It was a paraphrase from Shakespeare's *King Henry IV Part II,* when Falstaff says, "I am not only witty in myself, but the cause that is wit in others." As I stood there thinking about it, it occurred to me that Marty wasn't just being her usual clever self, but that she was paying me a great compliment.

The acid test for likeability is in the Shakespeare quote paraphrased in that birthday card Marty gave me: you make me like myself. In other words: If I like me when I'm with you, then I like you. Is this how you make others feel? Can you accomplish this by making a few changes in your likeability factors? If so, you will attain all the power associated with likeability. It's a valuable Shortcut—after all, most people describe their human Shortcuts as highly likeable. Conversely, if you make others feel bad about themselves or the situation when they're with you, the result will be strong negative feelings associated with you. Then, instead of being a successful Shortcut, you're the source of a struggle, and struggles take time; they create bottlenecks. If this is what you're experiencing, it's time to back up and review your likeability factors. What could you be doing differently?

One of the best ways for you to create the likeability Shortcut is to understand the people you are with and work to uphold their self-image. That lesson is coming up.

Exercise

Watch your favorite television program, preferably a competitive reality show like *American Idol, Survivor, The Biggest Loser,* or any other that highlights the rawness of humanity. As you watch, notice the characters you like and want to win versus those you don't like and want to lose. Which of the factors do the ones you like have going for them?

- Physical attractiveness

- Similarity

- Recognition and Complimenting

- Cooperation

Usually, people you like will have more than one of these attributes, and the more they have, the more you'll find you like them. Be as specific about the attributes you identify as you can. Now, what about the participants you dislike? What, in your mind, is missing that makes them unlikable to you? Why do they irritate you? Focus on the attributes listed here. Yes, there will be other factors that come into play that we haven't discussed, but you'll find most of what you need to know in these four. As you become more aware of what you like and dislike in these anonymous characters, you'll find you can be more honest about your own likeability factors.

Shortcut Lesson

The shortest distance between you and someone else is to like that person. One of the most magnetic, powerful things you can be is likeable. You become likeable when people like being around you; and they like being around you because they feel good about *themselves* when they are with you. That has to do with your ability to validate the good things they think and feel about themselves. To be liked, you have to first like. For some people that is a challenge, but it is a requirement of this Shortcut.

Image

Your Status Is Not Quo

> Treat others as if they were already who they wish
> they were.
>
> —Mohandas Gandhi

Your status is not quo; it changes when your audience changes. The more mastery you achieve in a particular area, the less significant the change in perception will be about you from situation to situation; but there will still be a shift.

I consider myself to be good at my job. I regularly address groups, both large and small, of businesspeople who are tops in their field. Despite their importance within their organizations, they (or their bosses) have hired me to offer help, support, and encouragement. I am a Shortcut for them, and I have achieved high "status" because they consider me to be accomplished in my area of expertise. I'm comfortable in front of my audiences; I have strong control of my subject matter; and I tailor my presentations to each audience.

One of the hallmark topics of my presentations is the brain and endocrine (hormone) science, which I delve into to explain certain behaviors and how it is possible to change them, if desired. I've studied a lot about this, reading anything I can get my hands on that addresses brain-based behavioral science. But given that I'm not a doctor, to ensure what I say is accurate, I have had several of my physician friends look over my work. Still I will never forget the day my audience was filled with neurosurgeons. The confidence I typically feel turned into gurgling mush in my belly before I spoke. My mastery or knowledge was no different with them than it had been with the previous group I'd addressed; the difference was the audience. So I had to recast my knowledge and experience—soft-pedal it. Fortunately, I knew beforehand who was going to be in the audience, and so I asked them during the first part of my talk to check my facts as I went along. I also expressed my desire to describe the science they understood so well in a different way than they might be used to, and concluded, "See what you think when I'm finished."

To accommodate the situation, I deliberately changed my status, from expert to "funny speaker-guy who needs your help." It worked; they were attentive, and only once was I corrected, on a minor detail. However, if I hadn't paid attention to who my audience was—in this case, neurosurgeons—my mastery would have likely been challenged, because I'm not one of them.

Keep in mind that as you're working on gaining mastery of a topic or skill, your accomplishments and professional reputation remain unchanged, as does your mastery or knowledge of the material. What does change is your status, from situation to situation; and to be a master Shortcut, you will have to adapt with it.

Let me quickly add here, when I say "status," I'm not referring to the prestige that comes from the kind of car you drive or the zip code you live in. I'm talking about who you are professionally, and where you and your skills fall in the pecking order. I'm also talking about how you are perceived—both by your audience and yourself.

None of us is exempt from what I call "status shift." It happens to the president of the United States when he goes from a press conference in the Rose Garden to a meeting with heads of state or to ask Congress to approve his budget. It happens to the car-wash guy, who behaves differently in front of his customers than when he's addressing his crew. The new woman in the IT department—fresh from completing classes on computer hardware maintenance—holds forth in a vigorous debate about a complicated data storage issue with her peers; but when the chief technology officer asks her about the same issues, she behaves completely differently—she's more deferential. Even the CEO of a multibillion-dollar corporation assumes one level of status in a meeting with his direct reports and another when he's presenting to major shareholders.

The point is that the image we have of ourselves is, in part, shaped by our audience; and Shortcuts are expert when it comes to this status shift, and when it comes to reading their audience. Though their mastery does not alter, they make the adjustments necessary to accommodate their audience.

Let's say you are an expert in finance, and you have been asked to talk to high school seniors who are interested in financial careers. The students will undoubtedly view you as a wise and battle-tested professional who knows just about everything there is to know about this subject area. Later, when you go back to the office and meet with a group of your professional peers, your level of knowledge won't have changed from when you were with the students, but the way you'll be perceived will. Later still, at the end of the day, you are asked to make a presentation to the chief financial officer. Your status changes again, even though your level of mastery stays relatively constant.

This might not seem intuitive; but if you think how good it feels when the image you have of yourself is acknowledged and applauded, you can understand the power and influence that comes when *you* are the one who is responsible for upholding others' images of themselves. You build professional strength when you spend time to get to know people well enough—to be so focused on their needs and who they are—that you can enforce the image they have of themselves.

Status is such a powerful thing in any society that when you seemingly give another person the upper hand by ceding your role, and understanding what they believe theirs to be, *you're* the one who is actually in the influencer's seat.

Jill, a woman in one of my workshops asked me during a break how she was ever going to get along with a coworker she "couldn't stand." She carried on about how awful this man was, how utterly impossible he was to work with. When I asked her about her options, she said that she had no choice but to work with him. So I told her that something I knew she didn't want to hear: "You will have to like him before you can like working with him." She told me there was nothing she could think of that was likeable about him, and continued to list all the reasons he was impossible to be around. As I listened, it occurred to me how difficult it is some-times—and how much effort it takes—to find something likeable about a person you have to work with, you can't fire, and who makes life miserable for you.

The plain fact is, it is not easy to like someone who makes us feel bad about ourselves—but it is *possible*. I suggested to Jill that she invite her coworker out for coffee, to get to know him on a more per-sonal level. Maybe by doing so she could find something out about his life that would help her to see him in a different light. She con-tinued to resist, and I was running out of break time to convince her that she either had to change the situation or put up with how bad it felt. Finally I understood that she believed the relationship would get mended only if she could sit him down and point out how *he* could make *her* feel better. So I gave her this assignment: "Your task in the next few weeks is to figure out how he wishes to be seen—not the positive-couched-in-a-negative view that we ascribe to people we don't like—but the positive, subjective view he has of himself."

Still she resisted. Finally I said, "Do you honestly believe that he thinks of himself the way you do? Do you suppose he thinks he's a jerk?" The lightbulb went on. She agreed then to take on the task of finding out about his positive image of himself. It would take some digging, but I was sure the time she spent doing it would make her work life much more agreeable.

Jill took her problematic colleague to breakfast, and told me at a subsequent workshop how it went. "I said to him, 'Though we work together a lot, I really don't know much about you.' He was a lit-tle surprised, and suspicious about the purpose of the meeting, but he did open up. I found out that he has two kids from a previous marriage whom he adores. He spends his spare time being a dad to them. He believes his most important job on earth is to make sure they are safe and that they end up becoming decent adults."

Jill said, "I was floored by this. I never figured him for a parent-type guy."

Based on this new information, Jill made some quick and accurate assessments about this man's positive self-image. She decided that, from that moment on, she would treat him as the great nurturer and parent he believed himself to be. She would ask him questions about how his kids were doing and make suggestions about fun activities she had done with her kids that his might enjoy as well.

In time, their relationship changed much for the better, because this man's status shifted in Jill's eyes. Who he truly was had always been there, but it hadn't come across in a work context; or at least not in a way that Jill had been willing to acknowledge. Once she started treating him in a way that harmonized with *how he viewed himself,* she became an ally, a confidante, and a respected colleague. Remember, the lesson of likeability is that you have to *first like to be liked.*

There are many lessons in image that can guide you as a Shortcut, and lead to Shortcuts for you to use. Roger Fisher and Daniel Shapiro have negotiated some of the world's most critical moments, from the Mideast Peace Accord talks of the 1970s to arms negotiations during the Cold War to corporate mergers and acquisitions. Their methods for quickly getting to the heart of the matter are brilliantly laid out in their excellent book, *Beyond Reason: Using Emotions to Negotiate.*[15] They discuss status in terms of understanding the role each person at the negotiation table believes that he or she is there to play. If you don't do your homework and understand the roles up front, positive progress can turn negative, in a hurry.

Have you ever been in a meeting when you or someone else essentially hijacked the agenda and twisted it into his or her own by directing the discussion to meet his or her needs? If so, you've witnessed the sometimes unknowing self-sabotage of taking over another person's role. You've seen the leader of the meeting start out as one person and lose his or her position halfway through when another person begins running the show. You walk out of the meeting unable to really explain what happened; but you and everyone else who was there knows it went badly. If you understand the role people believe they play when you go into a meeting, you can expertly respond to it and make sure you don't step on toes.

This illustrates how your status can change from situation to situation. Sometimes you're the meeting leader, sometimes you're the listener, and sometimes you're there to offer support. Your body of knowledge doesn't change, but your status shifts. Shortcuts understand that their status is dynamic. They do the homework to find out the possible roles of the various meeting members up front, and they create a Shortcut to ensure an excellent outcome.

Exercise

Answer these questions to get on the road to understanding image and status.

1. *What's your status?* Are you an expert at what you do? Are you a beginner? Or are you somewhere in the middle hoping to move up, or worried that you're sliding down? Your status—once you understand it—will still shift according to the audience you're in front of (even if you're a beginner at work, you're probably the expert with a group of teens, for example).

2. *Is your status high?* "I'm a great Shortcut." Write down all areas in your life—both personal and professional— where you'd comfortably make the claim that you're a

top Shortcut. Parenting, accounting, dog walking, managing, gardening—where do you have high status?

3. *Is your status low?* "I could be a better Shortcut." Write down all the areas where you find yourself taking a backseat to others. Why do you think you do this? Could better mastery take your status from low or medium to high?

4. *How can you have high status as a Shortcut?* Try this exercise: Before you go into a meeting with one or more colleagues or customers, prepare by asking yourself, "What role am I expected to play right now? What are others' roles? Are there going to be conflicting roles within this group (for example, two people who think they're in charge)? Can I be a valuable Shortcut by diffusing these conflicts?"

Shortcut Lesson

Shortcuts understand that mastery is not really a destination, and that you never actually arrive at this status. Achieving mastery is a path, a journey. The more knowledge you have on a topic, the easier it is to relate to various people on this topic. When you rest on your knowledge to get you through *all* situations, however, you'll find that it doesn't work with a particular group, or that someone knows more than you. Knowledge then becomes a neutralized asset; so being an expert is in the eyes of the beholder. Shortcuts work on the expertise aspect throughout their lives so that they can be prepared for more and more situations. Sometimes a situation has nothing to do with knowledge of a particular topic, but everything to do with knowledge of people; so understanding the people side of the equation is just as important.

When you understand the image others have of themselves, you have the opportunity to treat them as if they are who they think they are. All too often a confrontation has to do with someone seeking or needing validation in their role. People will spend an inordinate amount of time making sure that you agree with their position, how they see themselves, and their reasoning.

The Care and Feeding of Your Shanti

Nurturing Your Network of Shortcuts

> First you need only look: Notice and honor the radiance
> of Everything about you . . . Play in this universe. Tend
> all these shining things around you: The smallest plant,
> the creatures and objects in your care. Be gentle and
> nurture.
>
> —Anne Hillman
> *actress*

A physician friend of mine recalls his residency as perhaps the most grueling, intense, and exhausting phase of his life. During this period, he was a peer with two other medical students in residency, a couple named Scott and Shanti, who eventually married. They had double the number of issues to face of most other residents, because they were going through their individual programs at the same time. They recognized that if they didn't pay attention to their relationship, it wouldn't survive this focus-intensive time of their lives. So Scott came up with relationship rules he called the "Care and Feeding of Your Shanti." Not just rules for Scott to follow about Shanti, they went both ways. Here they are:

- Acknowledge and appreciate Shanti.

- Shanti appreciates good, healthful food. Feed Shanti well.

- Pamper Shanti.

- Don't be blameful.

- Keep Shanti smiling.

- Know when Shanti needs extra attention.

What does this have to do with Shortcuts? We have to take care of our "Shantis." I have this picture in my mind of the most influential people in the world. I see them sitting in their offices going through their old Rolodex card system and randomly making calls to their contacts—checking in, saying hello. These calls are short; they are simply a way to reach out. They are taking care of their Shantis—their Shortcuts. When they need something "right now," they rarely have to think about who to call on and how to approach that person to get what they need. They know exactly where to go on their short list of Shortcuts. And, the phone call they make to their Shortcuts isn't a surprise because they've been tending to them all along.

When you take care of your Shantis—your Shortcuts—they take care of you. Your Shortcuts do their stuff so that you can do your stuff. Your stuff is to be a Shortcut, as well. It bears repeating: *To be a Shortcut, you must have and use Shortcuts.* Nurture your Shantis.

One of the most skilled people I know at nurturing his network of Shantis is Mark Cornetta. His meteoric rise to president and general manager of one of the nation's most respected local television stations is a testament to many things; but along the way, Mark always knew who his Shortcuts—his Shantis—were. And he would probably agree that it was paying attention to his Shortcuts that enabled him to become such a good one himself.

To watch Mark in action when something needs to be done is akin to witnessing performance art, and is a textbook case of exactly how to nurture the ever-so-important life network we all need to survive and thrive in the world today. He can pick up the phone and, without awkwardness or a lot of cozying up, ask the Shortcut on the other end for something. And it's done without question. Of course, with his job, Mark is one of the best-connected businessmen in Denver, and possibly in the entire United States. But Mark does nothing different now than he did when he was in a job without all the glamour of his current position. When he was a sales representative for the stations for which he worked, he stayed connected; he nurtured his network. That is, he didn't call only when he needed something. He values his Shortcuts, so much so that most of them have become friends. He is one of the busiest people I know, and yet he calls me and takes the time for a quick breakfast or dinner—"just because." Mark has Shortcut relationships with his dry cleaners, his barber, his car repair service people, and so on. If you know Mark, you wouldn't be surprised to see him taking extra time with any one of these people. Mark has mastered influence by nurturing his Shortcuts, and by doing so, he has become one of the best executives in television management.

Sarah Michel, a dear personal friend and a speaker with a profound message, is another person who understands the importance of maintaining connections with one's network of Shortcuts. Sarah talks about "Connecting the Dots," and her idea is, simply, that your network affects your net worth. If managed well and nurtured properly, you can rely on this network in a variety of situations throughout your life.

A few years ago Sarah was diagnosed with Hodgkin's lymphoma, a cancer that had taken the lives of both her mother and her brother. Her sister was diagnosed, as well, two weeks after their mother was buried. Now, Sarah thought, I'm number four. She talks about the first week of her journey as she set out to learn her fate. She knew the symptoms for this form of cancer all too well, and she had them all; but still, she held out hope that maybe it was just a persistent cough.

From the beginning, she encountered a series of bottlenecks, which would have stymied even the most persistent among us. First, she had an MRI on a Friday, but was told "the diagnosis would have to wait until the next week because there was no one to look at her scan over the weekend." She picked up the phone and, with the help of a number of people in her network, had her MRI read within hours. She learned the tumor in her chest would require a biopsy. But, on Monday, her oncologist told her she would need to wait another week for surgery because of scheduling problems. But based on her family members' experiences, she knew that the tumor was capable of growing at an alarming rate, and she couldn't afford to wait a week. So she made a call. To even her oncologist's amazement, her surgery was scheduled for that Wednesday.

For the third time, Sarah hit a bottleneck. She was told there was no one available to interpret the pathology of the biopsy until the following week. Most mere mortals would have been daunted by this series of events, but Sarah is a master networker—it's her life. She makes a living by teaching people how to do it. So she brought her considerable skills into play to, literally, save her life. Within a week, she had an MRI performed and interpreted, a biopsy surgery performed and interpreted, and she started on chemotherapy—all of which would have taken at least three weeks in the best of circumstances. But Sarah knows people who know people who know people. Every time she met with a "wait and see" response, Sarah picked up the phone and contacted her network— her Shantis. And it worked. It was as if an entire universe of Sarah-supporters were heralded to come to her aid.

Like Mark, Sarah pays attention to her network. She might not talk with some of her Shortcuts for months, or even years; but she stays connected with the inner circle of that network; and by doing so she saved her life. Today, both Sarah and her sister enjoy cancer-free lives.

TACTICS TO NURTURE AND GROW YOUR SHORTCUT NETWORK

LinkedIn.com is one of my favorite sites on the Internet. It's like Facebook.com or MySpace.com, but for professionals who want to nurture their Shortcuts. You go online, sign up, and begin linking to college friends you haven't spoken to in a long time but with whom you blew beer out of your nose in 1978. You link to former coworkers, no matter how long ago you lost track of them, and no matter where they are. If they are on LinkedIn.com, and you have entered your work experience and education data into the forms, you can find these people and rekindle the magic you had with them when they were present in your life. The big bonus is that you also become linked to the people they are linked to. This second tier of contacts now become acquaintances through a sort of cyber "Oh-yeah-I-know-Steve-too-how-do-you-know-him?" kind of connection. There's even a third tier, of those who are linked to the second tier. In my own case, thanks to the more than 200 people I am currently linked to, I have a reach of about 14,000 people through my second tier, and a whopping 1.5 million people through the third tier. This is Shortcut-tending on steroids, if you do it right.

When I first went onto LinkedIn.com, at the urging of a client who was already on it, I couldn't believe how much fun I could have inviting people back into my life. What is even more fun is how excited they usually are that we're connected again. As I become reacquainted with these people and what they do, my Shortcut list has grown, and life is very good. It has taught me to take care of those who take care of me.

Let me share with you how a certain Shortcut in my life works for me. It's very simple. My great friend, Realtor Nancy Brauer, has been part of my life for about 15 years now. She has helped me find a few houses during the time we have known each other. Before I bought the house I currently live in, she talked me out of buying a different house. Either I wasn't ready, she would say, or the market wasn't ready. She kept telling me, "When it's time, it's time, and it's not time." That went on for about three years—think about it, a realtor talking someone out of spending money with her.

My trust level for her went sky high. She helped me get into the great house I now live in. One of the things I learned during the inspection of the house was that the roof would need to be replaced. So I negotiated a bit of money for that, and planned to replace the roof when the time came. Well, the time came just a few months after I moved in. I called Nancy and asked, "If you were replacing your roof, who would you ask to do it?" She said,

"Bernie Reitz, hands down. He's a little expensive, but well worth the investment."

Well, I knew I wanted the roof to be classy and high quality, so I called Bernie and got an estimate—not an estimate for the faint of heart, mind you. What Bernie didn't know was that I wasn't bidding him against any other roofer. Why? Because one of my Shortcuts had already done the homework over her years in the real estate market and had become an expert in all things related to home maintenance and repair. She was my Shortcut. She was my go-to person. And if you asked me today for the name of a Realtor, Nancy Brauer is the name I would give you. Incidentally, she just retired, so her Realtor recommendation to her clients and friends like me will be worth millions to the lucky few Nancy dubs to be queen of her sphere. That's how influential Shortcuts become in our lives.

It's important to nurture out network of "Nancys" because they give us the freedom to become the Shortcut we wish to be. Do the following exercise; it will give you clues about how you want to be perceived as a Shortcut. But, first, think about the Shortcuts you currently use.

Exercise

With your favorite Shortcut in mind, list three to five attributes that make him or her a great Shortcut:

1.

2.

3.

4.

5.

Next list three to five ways this Shortcut makes you *feel*:

1.

2.

3.

4.

5.

Now take the list of those "back-room" people from the "Unload the Overload" chapter. They are your Shortcuts. Take a few minutes and think how you'll deliberately take care of them. For example, I send a simple "thinking about you" e-mail to my Shortcuts. I try to send about five a week, one per day. If you're a high achiever, you can send handwritten notes. Nothing says "I care about you" more than that. There are countless small things you can do to stay connected. Get deliberate about it. Use the chart here to fill your thoughts:

Who are your shortcuts?	What will you do for them?
1.	
2.	
3.	
4.	
5.	
6.	
7.	

Exercise (Continued)

We all have Nancys—Shantis—in our lives, and we all have the capability to be a Nancy for others. When you find the Nancys in your life, cherish and nurture them, just as you would wish someone would do for you. Your Shortcuts will take care of you if you take deliberate action and do simple things that reach out to your Shortcuts. And by doing so, you're actively applying the glue that keeps your network together. It feels great, too.

Shortcut Lesson

When you're in a pinch and need something right away, if you have a nice list of Shortcuts that you have been nurturing, you'll be able to rely on them to get you what you need. They are your Shortcuts—your Nancys and Shantis; and because you have taken care of them, they will take care of you. When they do, they free you up to become the Shortcut you wish to be. It is the care and feeding of your Shortcuts that makes all the difference in the world.

Attitude

Why a Good Attitude Will Make You Money, and a Bad One Will Cost You

A positive attitude may not solve all your problems, but it will annoy enough people to make it worth the effort.

—HERM ALBRIGHT
writer for the Saturday Evening Post

Remember the discussion earlier about the high-maintenance employee? If you come with an attitude—a bad one, that is— you become one. There are few things more certain than the fact that you will repel others—even if you are brilliant and skilled—if you have a nasty disposition or a negative attitude. A whole body of psychology, called emotional intelligence, has been created around this premise. Research psychologists looked around at all of the derailed high-IQ, "high-functioning" people and asked why so many had failed in their careers—and, often, in their personal lives as well. They then asked why people with more modest intellectual capabilities often succeeded dramatically. The answer, they discovered, lay in so-called noncognitive competencies, skills that are not about thinking, but rather about emotions and the management of them.

We all know the tech guy (insert any highly skilled professional here, not just tech people!) who, when we have to call and ask him to fix our computer, makes us feel like a complete and utter idiot. He usually clicks a few keys, goes to some mysterious file in our computer that we never knew existed, hits the Enter button, and then reboots. Voilá! the problem is gone. Yes, some of these guys truly are geniuses. But often they also look at us like we should stop being fed because we cannot figure out on our own how to fix such obviously easy (to them) problems.

I used to hate having to get on the phone with a computer tech when my laptop needed fixing. After wading through the jungle of phone tree branches to get to the music that would finally lead me to someone who would probably pass me on to someone else, the tension built up in me could be sliced with a butter knife. Still, I maintained Pollyanna-esque delusions that those techs would understand that I had just taken what felt like a quarter of my adult life to reach them to address my simple but very important question, and that, therefore, they would be sensitive to my frustration and not speak to me in a condescending way. Wrong. Instead of acknowledging or apologizing for the excessive wait-time I had just experienced, they jumped right into their interrogation of all my secret passwords and codes, to confirm that I did indeed own one of their products. Once we were past that, the test of knowledge began—at which point I became frustrated. I'm not a computer expert and I don't know all the language, so I always became tongue-tied. And all of a sudden, that serious problem I called about, the one that had grown with each moment I spent on hold, seemed trivial. Nevertheless, I still needed it fixed. So Mister Computer Smarty Pants took me through some *Harry Potter* incantations. When that didn't work, *he* started getting frustrated and talking down to me. I thought these guys were supposed to be Shortcuts! Eventually, we would get it resolved—or as happened twice, I had to ship my computer to them!

Then one day, someone looked at experiences like mine (and, I'm guessing, yours as well) and thought, "Hmmm. Let's see if the combination of smart *and* nice can work in the technical customer service area." Enter the thriving Shortcut business that has blossomed: The Geek Squad. The techs on the squad even have their own painted Volkswagen Bugs. They demonstrate exactly what a Shortcut should be, at the same time they capitalized on a widespread need and extraordinarily high-cost (excessive amounts of time on the phone) service. They turned it into a low-cost service (in terms of both time and money), and the business prospers because of it. And perhaps most importantly, the Shortcut they provide to customers is that they do their jobs with a friendly, helpful attitude.

Another reason that attitude is so critical to success is that it leaves people with a feeling, either good or bad. They might not be able to articulate why they feel one way or the other after an experience with you, but the feeling is there, nonetheless. The more you can direct that feeling in a positive direction through your attitude and your approach, the more likely it is that you'll create good experiences. We have all heard tales of the legendary service Nordstrom has provided its clientele over the years. I used to wonder aloud to friends, "How could it be that big a deal? It's just a department store." Then I went into a Nordstrom. The staff there actually paid attention to me, whether I bought something or not. They created an experience that made me want to come back.

A dramatic example of this came not too long ago when I went into the newly opened Nordstrom in Denver's posh Cherry Creek shopping center. I'm not sure what exactly possessed me to step foot into a mall during one of the busiest holiday weeks of the year, but I did; and I was murmuring under my breath that little shopper's prayer: "Please, dear Lord, help me to keep my wits about me, even when people keep bumping into me, walk at a snail's pace in front of my hurried feet, and while overwrought mothers and fathers scream at their children that Santa is not going to bring them anything if they don't shape up." I successfully serpented my way to the Nordstrom store in the mall; it was around lunchtime. I went up to its Bistro to get something to eat, my spirits falling further as I noticed yet another line of people oozing out the restaurant's entrance. I decided to wait. I had no energy to "go out there again."

More quickly than I would have hoped, I made it to the front of the line and was seated at the dining bar. Sanctuary. I thought, "Wow, that prayer thing really worked." The servers at this extraordinarily high-volume Bistro carried on with the legendary Nordstrom service. They made me feel as if I were the only one they were serving, and that my needs were the most important in the world. When I asked the busy busboy for ketchup, he immediately stopped what he was doing and made a beeline to get me some. I only spent $15 for my meal, but I left feeling as if I had been in the world's fanciest restaurant and had ordered their Beluga caviar. I was ready to face the mall again. And I knew that no matter what happened to me in the shopping-war zone, as I wended my way back to the other end of the mall, the afterglow of my Nordstrom experience would carry me through

The feeling that people have when they've been in your presence predicts a lot about what they'll think about you. If you're smart and nasty (or, to use the Nordstrom metaphor: If you have all the best merchandise in the world, but your staff is snooty), few people will return for seconds. Successful Shortcuts want to increase their value by becoming the resource that people think of every time. It *does* matter how people feel about you. It's not just your knowledge. Ask yourself: How do you leave people feeling after you've "served" them? Do they feel as if it was *your* honor to be able to serve them; or do they feel as if *they* should be honored that you stopped during your busy day to accommodate them? Think about that. The answer to those questions will tell you a lot about yourself as a Shortcut. It's just a feeling—but it makes all the difference in the world.

Shortcut Lesson

Here's what the world has to say to those who are stuck in the old mode of service, like the pre-Geek Squad people: First, if we knew how to do it, we'd do it ourselves and there would be no need for you. Second, people fail because they don't

behave well in the world. Third—and here's the big lesson—
you can prosper quite handsomely by taking a highly needed
service and transforming it into a great customer experience
just by improving the attitude of the people providing the
service.

Attitude creates an experience. Good or bad. You choose.
The bad one nearly always costs you.

Emotional Intelligence

The Must-Have Trait of a Shortcut

> In the past, we used to reward the lone rangers in the
> corner offices because their achievements were brilliant
> even though their behavior was destructive. That day is
> gone. We need people who are better at persuading than
> at barking orders, who know how to coach and build
> consensus. Today, managers add value by brokering with
> people.
>
> —LARRY BOSSIDY
> *former chairman and CEO AlliedSignal*

You can pile up all the advanced degrees and certifications in the
world, and if you don't know how to interact with other people—
how to share what you know to make others' lives easier—you will
eventually be a victim of your own intellect. You may be smart on
paper, but you have a lot to learn in another area.

Dr. Reuven Bar-On is one of the world's seminal research-
ers on emotional intelligence. He uses what he calls the EQ-i, to
determine how much of it a person has. His layperson definition
of emotional intelligence is that it is the measurement of street
smarts, of experiential wisdom. His more academic definition, as
detailed in the *EQ-i BarOn Emotional Quotient Inventory Technical
Manual*[16] is as follows:

> Emotional Intelligence is concerned with understand-
> ing oneself and others, relating to people, and adapting
> to and coping with immediate surroundings in order

144

to be more successful in dealing with environmental demands.

Emotional Intelligence is tactical, and deals with immediate functioning (arguments, reprimands, praising, and so on) while IQ (cognitive intelligence) deals with long-term capacity (strategic planning, forecasting, budgeting, and so on).

Emotional Intelligence helps to predict success because it reflects how a person applies knowledge to the immediate situation. In a way, to measure emotional intelligence is to measure one's common sense and ability to get along in the world.

Put in Shortcut language, there are attractor behaviors and repeller behaviors. Attractor behaviors are the ones that cause others to want to be in your presence. They're enlarging and engaging; they create a feeling of safety, and they usually make others feel good overall. Repeller behaviors are those that diminish, and often cause anger or fear. They're unpleasant, and usually make others feel bad, about you and, sometimes, themselves. The more your attractor behaviors come into play, the more people will want to be around and support you—and vice versa.

Unfortunately, all too often, we forget to put our attractor behaviors into action. We get so busy with our day-to-day demands and the volume of our work that we become a little numb. The result is that we become used to feeling, at the very least, neutral, if not bad, about other people, including those to whom we are supposed to provide a service (such as a boss, a customer, a colleague). We accept those less than optimum feelings and rarely question how emotion figures into our state of being—until there is a crisis. Then—depending on the situation, whether another person makes us feel bad, or vice versa—there is usually a messy conflict, or even an all-out confrontation.

Exercise

Ask yourself:

- How do people feel after they've been around you? Do they feel good or bad? What about you? Do you feel good or bad?

- How do you treat others when you are having a bad day or facing negative circumstances?

The simplicity of these questions seems to take many people aback—possibly because they are so basic, and we seem to assign a higher degree of credibility to things that are complex. But I encourage you to do this "gut-check"; it does work

Let's say you've been charged with preparing a report for your department, which is due to your boss every Wednesday. (You are a Shortcut for your boss, after all, and compiling this report improves his workflow.) Before you can write this report, however, you have to gather input from all the other people in your department—which, lately, admit it, you've been doing in a less-than-gracious way. Although, truth be told, you haven't really been conscious about how you go about soliciting this input; you consider it their job to get it to you when you need it— which is Tuesdays, so you have a day to write the report. Yet for two years, every week, you've been sending out a last-minute, semi-nagging e-mail reminding your colleagues you need their numbers and analyses on your desk by the end of the day. You don't follow up with a personal reminder, you don't use humor—"that's not businesslike," you think—and you rarely remember to thank anyone for helping you pull this report together.

Little do you know that when your colleagues see that e-mail, some of them go into "neutral" gear: "Oh, him again; I've got other things to get done first"; or they're all-out peeved: "Oh, *him again*! I'm sick of getting this last-minute request every week. Anyway, it's work he should be doing himself! If last minute is good enough for him, it's good enough for me. He'll get it last minute."

Now consider what would happen if you applied a little emotional intelligence to the situation. How do you want others to feel about you? About themselves? Imagine if you reworded your e-mail, sent it out a day earlier, then took a few minutes to stop by the desks of your colleagues to say, "Hey, thanks for getting me the numbers—I know it's a pain, but I know you understand that it's something we have to do. Which reminds me, I wonder if you have some suggestions for improving how we gather the data and do this report—I'd love to hear your thoughts. There's got to be an easier way, one that doesn't cause such a disruption for everyone. It always feels as if we're always doing fire drills, and that's not good for any of us."

See the difference? All it takes is a few well-placed words of acknowledgment and collaboration. In contrast, the "it's-your-job-so-I-shouldn't-have-to-thank-you-for-it" approach will rarely get you far. But by providing intelligence to the emotional side of such situations, almost without fail you'll find people are willing to go above and beyond for you; they will want to make you look good. And don't overlook another, underlying, lesson here: Don't be a Shortcut just for your boss; be a Shortcut for your colleagues, too. They'll love you for it.

An aspect of emotional intelligence is a concept called emotional knowledge. In its simplest form, this means knowing what comes next in the sequence of emotions. If I am outwardly angry at you, using harsh words and a loud voice, I can expect a few probable emotional reactions from you. Imagine how you would feel if I shouted the following statement at you:

"You idiot! How could you be so incredibly ignorant! Of course, I needed the report today! What part of, 'I need it today' don't you understand?!"

You would likely feel defensiveness, angry, anxious, and perhaps even fearful.

What if, instead, although I was angry, I managed to measure my words, taking into account how you would feel about my anger directed toward you? Compare how you felt about the preceding statement with this alternative:

"Oh, gosh [said with exasperation]; I probably wasn't very clear about when I needed this report. I'm going to have to work some magic to get it ready for the boss on time. Okay; this is a priority now. I'll need your help with it."

Perhaps you'd feel remorse, anxiety, or disappointment in yourself. But whereas the first set of emotions would probably lead to shutdown and/or defensive behavior, the second set most likely would lead to only a temporary shutdown, followed by quick recovery and action.

Shortcuts take into account and incorporate this fascinating body of emotional knowledge into their lives. They know that their intellectual capabilities will be sabotaged by negative emotional outbursts, which only serve to take them from Shortcut to bottleneck in a matter of a few words.

In 1980, psychologist Robert Plutchik published a fascinating study on the evolution of emotions. His groundbreaking work, "A General Psychoevolutionary Theory of Emotion," published in *Emotions and Life: Perspectives from Psychology, Biology, and Evolution*[17] beautifully describes the paths of human emotion. Take a look at his illustration of how one emotion can reasonably lead to the next.

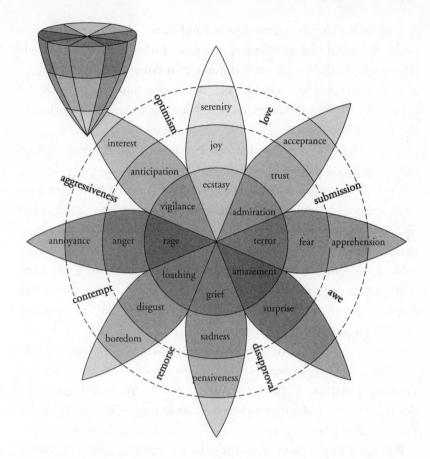

You don't need a degree in psychology to recognize that minor emotions, left unchecked or fueled by ignorance of yourself and others, can lead to major, negative ones. Therein lies the crux of emotional intelligence. To be a successful Shortcut, it's essential to work on this aspect of yourself as much—or more than—the expertise part. Let's take a look at how understanding emotions can make all the difference.

Assume for this example that you're a technician whose job it is to help people over the telephone. Also assume that you're aware how many people would rather slam their finger in a door than go through the machinations required to place a tech call. Third, assume you realize that by the time they call, customers are usually frustrated to begin with, and so may not be able to articulate as clearly as you'd like them to. Finally, assume that most customers who get you on the phone are not aware (and wouldn't care, even if they were) that you are rewarded by your company for the speed at which you handle each call; they are interested only in having their problems taken care of, no matter how long it takes. If, in this job, you forget to do the aforementioned gut-check or to keep in mind the assumptions just described, instead approaching customers' problems without genuine consideration for their feelings, the experience will be negative from the get-go, and you will have an uphill battle on your hands. Your worth as a Shortcut will begin to diminish immediately. According to the Plutchik model, this experience could go from annoyance to rage in short order. If, however, you stay alert and pay attention to your gut, and the excellent assumptions it leads you to make, the response you generate will probably move from annoyance or frustration to calm and gratitude. It's all about shifting emotions from negative to positive.

There are many methods of changing a situation from bad to good, but one of the surest ways is to listen. *Really* listen. If a customer (or anyone) sounds angry, first acknowledge his or her feeling, saying for example: "I know these kinds of problems can be so frustrating; I hate when they happen to me, too." Or, if they sound anxious or unable to articulate their issue, help them: "Let's start at the beginning. Why don't I just ask you a few questions so that I get a good understanding of your problem." These kinds of approaches work well to get the customer "out of the rafters" and down on the ground so that you can demonstrate your value as a Shortcut to them. All it takes is listening for and understanding the emotions behind the words—and being aware of what might happen if you ignore them.

I recently made a much-dreaded phone call to Microsoft about a major software problem I was having. I suspected my machine might have a virus; it was entirely dysfunctional. I worked through the phone tree, which to Microsoft's credit was brief; I reached a live person quickly. The technician immediately introduced herself, gave me her name and a number I could call back if we got disconnected. She also gave me a case code so that, going forward, anyone in tech support at Microsoft could look up my file and help me, should the problem recur. In those 45 seconds or so, my anxiety quickly dropped down to a tolerable level, and I actually felt hope.

Here's how the rest of the 11-minute conversation went (I checked the elapsed time on my phone when I hung up, because I was so stunned that resolving my problem didn't take half a day):

> "Scott, please describe to me what is the main problem."
>
> I did.
>
> "There are many reasons that this could happen," she continued. At this point, I was ready for the brush-off, her telling me to contact the maker of the computer. Instead, she said, "Let's go through a process of elimination and see if we can get this cleared up, so you can be on your way. May I take control of your computer via remote access?"
>
> I agreed, and went through the process to allow her to tinker in my system while I, essentially, stood by.
>
> Notably, as she worked, she explained to me what she was doing. In a matter of minutes she found the culprit and explained to me how I could avoid it happening in the future.
>
> My computer was working again, and I was overjoyed. I also came away very impressed with Microsoft and it's tech support service.

Mind you, that isn't the experience I used to have with the company. In the past, techs there were negative, even abrasive, and would make me feel utterly stupid for having called. Even with the advent of the remote-access assistance—a brilliant Shortcut, by the way!—I still would sense the brush-off, leaving me clueless as to how to help myself in the future. The difference between my past scenarios and the one I just described here was not the skill or computer expertise of the tech; it was her emotional intelligence.

Shortcuts pay attention to the subtleties of emotion to make experiences successful. They're not just enamored with their own knowledge; they recognize intuitively that everyone wants to be around people who make us feel good, smart, validated—and like we're not going crazy for having asked a question.

As described in the previous chapter, positive attitude is an important part of being an excellent Shortcut, because a bad attitude creates a bottleneck, and requires a lot of defenses and skills to maneuver around—it takes us more time to get where we're going. That said, fast is not always better, or what's required. Over a long period of repeated exposure, given the choice between a quick journey led by an expert with a nasty attitude and a slightly slower journey directed by someone less proficient but more pleasant, most of us would opt for the latter. Shortcuts make us feel like our request is sane, valid, valued, and important.

In sum, if you want to sigh and huff and puff and bring grief to all of those around you, just know that your career will probably be short-lived. The common sense around this says no one likes to be in the company of mean-spirited, ill-willed, bad-tempered, and I've-got-a-dark-cloud-over-me-everywhere-I-go kind of people.

Shortcut Lesson

Shortcuts have a good attitude—good emotional intelligence. They make it easy to be around them. They make others *want* to be around them. They don't require the extra time to deal with them that bottlenecks do. Having and keeping a good attitude is a lot more difficult than you might think, however. But when people are relying on you everyday, unless something is catastrophic, they're too busy with their own "stuff" to have to deal with yours, too.

Focus

Finding What Motivates You

> The only lifelong, reliable motivations are those that
> come from within, and one of the strongest of those is
> the joy and pride that grow from knowing that you've
> just done something as well as you can do it.
>
> —LLOYD DOBYNS
> *author,* Thinking About Quality

If I were your boss and I offered you a bonus of 5 percent of your total quarterly salary to increase productivity in some aspect in your job, would you be motivated to do so? The answer in workshops I conduct is a resounding yes! Now let me put it another way to help you understand a bit about human motivation, and how it works both from the inside out and the outside in.

I once had two remarkable blond Labrador retriever sisters, Dot and Betty. They were smart, and like most other Labs, they loved to eat. I decided to use that to my advantage. Since Dot was the one with a real appreciation of food, I chose her as the one I would teach, when she was a puppy, to get the newspaper for me every morning. Betty would sit as sentinel when Dot ran down the driveway to retrieve the newspaper. To train Dot, I would lead her to the newspaper, hold it in her mouth as I walked her back to the house, all the while praising her to high heaven; then I would feed both dogs the moment we got back in the house. It worked—for a few weeks, anyway. Then one day when I opened the door, Betty took her customary perch on the porch and Dot raced to the end of the driveway; but she came back without the newspaper. It was the first time the paperboy had put a rain bag on it, and to Dot that didn't qualify as a newspaper. So I brought the dogs into the house and went to my computer and began to work. The dogs were baffled, and a little agitated. Where was their food? Eventually, Dot seemed to figure out what I was up to and nudged my knee while I sat at my desk. I opened the front door again, and this time Dot ran and fetched the newspaper.

The question here is the same as the salary bonus question I just posed: Who gets motivated, and for what reason? Is Dot motivated to get the newspaper? The answer is no. Dogs don't read newspapers. Dot is motivated to get the newspaper to get her food; likewise, employees are motivated to do more work to make more money. These are examples of extrinsic, or external, motivation; and it is a tactic that works.

But what if the motivator goes away or the value of the motivation is diminished? Uh oh! Suddenly a motivation barrier is erected. In contrast, Shortcuts figure out what motivates them *internally*, and that's what they use as their engine to keep on going, even when they don't feel like it.

Frederick Herzberg and David McClelland[18] were research psychologists whose theories and studies have been incorporated into nearly all of the most successful leadership and personal growth approaches over the last 50 years. One of these theories is the idea that the things that motivate us are not the same things that demotivate us. Let's take money, as an example, something that is usually hailed as a powerful motivator. Herzberg discovered that this is not necessarily true. Money is certainly an effective short-term motivator, so if you need quick bursts of activity for some purpose, then throw money at it. But in the long term, things tend to fall apart when money is all that is being applied to create motivation. Herzberg also noted, as early as 1968, in an article in the *Harvard Business Review*[19] that the lack of money was a demotivator. If, say an employer pays her people below par, they will ruminate about this injustice and in time become demotivated. Interestingly, however, Herzberg also found that when money was on par or slightly above it, people did not consider it a motivator; they didn't put it on their list of things that motivated them. From this Herzberg concluded that an entire class of people in the workforce was focused on the demotivators. He called these workers "maintenance-seekers." Some of the things they focus on are:

- Economics (pay and benefits)

- Physical space (cubicles, offices, parking spaces)

- Fairness (equal-opportunity job postings, rules)

- Social activities (Friday pizza parties, dress-down day)

In other words, there are millions of workers out there who spend an enormous amount of energy on things outside of their actual work duties.

The Shortcut, on the other hand, is very different. The Shortcut is a "motivation-seeker." Herzberg says workers who fall into this category are driven primarily by internal motivators, such as:

- Achievements/accomplishments at work

- Earned recognition (the feeling of pride is internal)

- The work itself

- Personal growth

- Advancement in the organization (paired with achievement)

- Responsibility

These are the traits of the Shortcuts. They have a very different focus and very different attitudes from those who are mainly concerned about demotivator issues. When an organization is filled with motivation-seeking people, it produces an uplifting and collaborative environment. When the maintenance-seekers reign, the result is typically an atmosphere of mistrust and cover-your-backside, one where finger-pointing is rampant.

Exercise

Review the two lists of maintenance-seeker and motivation-seeker attributes. Most of us are driven by a combination of both. On these lists, circle your primary maintenance and motivation issues. This will help to clarify your internal drivers (Shortcut drivers), versus those that rely upon others and outside forces. Keep in mind, there is no shame in having maintenance issues. If you take the time and effort to understand what they are, and learn how to clear them up, then you can begin to focus on the more positive motivation factors that will make you stand apart from the rest.

You may also use this exercise to analyze employees who work for you. You will gain excellent insight into how they work if you make accurate assumptions from both of the lists. In workshops, I encourage managers to do this, and to follow it up by having a discussion with their employees. I suggest that they introduce their employees to the lists, and ask them to perform the same exercises that they've done—to circle the maintenance and motivation attributes that apply to them. It's an ideal discussion-starter, and it brings about new understanding between the manager and the employee.

Shortcut Lesson

Shortcuts are focused on those attributes that make individuals and organizations come alive and thrive: intrinsic motivators. Examine any decaying organization and you will see that most of the people there are focused on maintenance issues. Businesses that excel and attract the best talent are staffed by individuals who are intent on the motivators. It's a snowball effect, and the momentum can take you and your company either way.

Meaning

Making Meaning, Not Making Money
(Though That's Nice, Too)

> I would rather die a meaningful death than live a
> meaningless life.
>
> —CORAZON AQUINO
> *president of the Philippines, 1986–1992*

A well-respected and uncannily wise colleague of mine, Mark Sanborn, taught me a very valuable lesson early in my speaking career. He said that professional speakers who have "arrived" have moved their professional intent from making money to making meaning. The money follows. I always thought this sounded profound, but I didn't grasp the depth of what Mark said until years later, when I realized it's the crux of the Shortcut philosophy. It's also a concept social science has given some teeth.

Dr. Martin Seligman touches on this subject by teaching the basis of inherited strengths that play out in our lives.[20] I listened first-hand during a semester-long class he taught on happiness and positive psychology. In it, he explained many things that reverberated through my very core; but one concept in particular I want to mention here is that psychologists have distinguished levels in our work-life: job, career, calling, and mission. Upon examination of these four levels, I came to two conclusions. First, there is a level at which Shortcuts dwell; second, at that level, it's mostly about making meaning, not making money.

The first level is the *job*. When I was earning money during high school, I worked as a sales clerk in a clothing store and as a busboy and server in a few different restaurants. It wouldn't have mattered if it was a tux shop or a jeans store, a Burger King, McDonald's, or a local diner—I just wanted to make money to fund my fun; that's all there was to it. That's a job, whose main purpose is to earn the worker the money to do the things he or she really wants to do.

Many people in the workforce work at jobs. I'm not passing judgment here; this is not about good or bad. What I am saying is that few people who work at jobs reach true Shortcut status. They may perform well and be an excellent resource in their job, but the job isn't a way of being or of living; it is just something to do to earn money. Real Shortcuts keep on going in their search for meaningful work.

Ask yourself if what you do currently is little more than a way for you to earn a paycheck. If it offers little or no long-lasting fulfillment, then you have an opportunity to start taking inventory of your life, to discover whether you can find work that will also bring meaning to your life. *That* is when you can begin to excel.

The next level is the *career*. This is where the majority of professionals find themselves. To be sure, a career can be a wonderful undertaking. It typically comprises a series of related jobs, strung together over a long period of time, sometimes even a lifetime. Millions of people out there enjoy successful and fulfilling careers. But what separates a career from the next level, a calling, is that many people are not completely satisfied in their current job. Once the newness of it fades, they begin to think about and prepare for the next job move in their career. Upward movement is incredibly important at this level; if there is none, the career stalls, and the career holder becomes disenchanted.

My first career was in television. There were many things about it that I truly loved. But there was an equal amount, if not more, of elements that bugged me to no end. Consequently, I was always searching for the next "best thing" in television. I was never truly satisfied. I did well, and won respect and some awards; but none of that kindled a fire in my belly. First I was an associate news producer, next a full producer, then a sports producer; after that I was a documentary writer and producer, followed by a stint as on-air talent coach; then I was a coach for executives who needed preparation for media blitzes and public talks.

It took a 10-year career in television to get me to the next level, my *calling*—and that is the level at which the Shortcut flourishes.

Don't misunderstand: I'm happy I went through my various career "jobs." I made great friends and have wonderful memories. I also developed incomparable skills, and I now know I had to take those career steps to get me to my calling. I didn't know that at the time, however. So if you're reading this and you're in a career that has begun to pale for you, and you yearn to make it to the Shortcut level, let the morphing begin.

The *calling* is the level to which most of us aspire, but one that remains elusive for so many. We've all met people who have found their calling, and we know this because they are at peace. We see them using their expertise to serve others, and they do it with happiness and great skill. The calling is a place to which you are drawn. It's where your inherited strengths manifest. You can't really get promoted in your calling, but you work your entire life to make yourself better in it. You will experience different iterations of your calling, but it's where you will be for the rest of your life, because you will be fulfilled there. You will be a Shortcut.

The calling is where your talents and skills flourish. You will feel you *have* to be there. And, interestingly, although the salary is not the top priority for people who have found their calling, often they are paid at top levels because they continually become better in it.

My sister Meg is a good example. She found her calling in forestry some 20 years ago, after having been a chef, the owner of a catering business, and a restaurant owner. She put herself through four years of university while running her business to pay for school. When she graduated, she was in her early forties, after which she took a job with the Colorado State Forest Service. Today, she loves what she does. She thrives at it. It took her years to find her calling, but when she did, she applied herself the way all successful Shortcuts do: she made the sacrifices, and dedicated herself to the effort with passion, and not a whole lot of thought about how rich she would become. Meg doesn't make tons of money; she doesn't even make pounds of money. But money isn't her driving force; her passion for what she does, is.

The same is often true for teachers, nurses, small business owners, and other fulfilled souls who work with a great love for what they do. They're often not in the money, but they are in their calling; and I've met many a wandering trust-funder who envies the person who has found his or her calling.

The fourth level, the *mission*, is the calling on steroids. It is where many of the world's philanthropists reign. Bill Gates, Warren Buffett, Andrew Carnegie, and the Rockefellers are a few who made it their life's missions to stand behind a cause—and had the necessary resources to back them. Most of us won't have the opportunity to live in this hallowed space, but it's sure worth dreaming about. Mind you, missionaries aren't necessarily rich people doing "good things," as we all know. Think Mother Theresa, Gandhi, Martin Luther King, and countless others whose mission it was to change the world for the better. It is impossible to put a dollar amount on the good that each of these people and others of their ilk over the centuries have done for the world.

Shortcut Lesson

There are different stages, or seasons, in your life's work. Sometimes you're in it for the money, and sometimes you're in it for the meaning; sometimes you're in it for both. As you ascend the ladder from job to career to calling and mission, you will experience greater work fulfillment. Figure out what stage you are in, then decide if it's where you want to be. If not, get on the journey of a Shortcut. Work to become the best at what you wish to do, and learn how to be an extraordinary human being while doing it.

Humor: The Secret Weapon of Shortcuts Everywhere

We awaken in others the same attitude of mind we hold toward them.

—ELBERT HUBBARD
American editor, publisher, and writer

Mary Beth is a United Airlines gate agent in Minneapolis. On September 20, 2007, a runway at Minneapolis International Airport was shut down for repair work. Add to that the unpredictable Midwest weather, mechanical issues with aircraft, the slowdown of Northwest Airlines (which hubs out of Minneapolis), and rush-hour traffic at the airport—and the result is chaos. You have irritated-beyond-reason passengers. You have frenzied, curt airline staff. Surrounding everything and everyone is negative energy.

Enter Mary Beth. Instead of blaming the madness on conditions beyond the airline's control, thus only encouraging the mental pushback and arguments from passengers, she diffused the situation with lightness, grace, and her own brand of Midwestern charm.

"It's an understatement to say that we're confused here at United today, so listen up so no one adds to the confusion," said Mary Beth loudly and with good humor over the intercom. "We're going to do everything we can to unravel all of this; in the meantime, listen for my perky announcements. I'm going to tell you everything I know, I promise. In return, please, please, *please* do not crowd the desk to ask where you are on the standby list of

182 people all going to Denver or Chicago. It'll just slow us way down. I'd like to ask that you continue, or at least start, to show your patience by ditching the grumpy attitude when you approach the desk. We'll return the favor."

The passengers in the waiting area burst into smiles and giggles. The tension was relieved. The blame was "rightfully taken," and Mary Beth illustrated what an excellent example of a Shortcut looks like. She uses her considerable expertise and personal abilities to make a complicated process work more smoothly—even when chaos threatens to break it all apart.

Shortcut Lesson

Shortcuts take responsibility; they resist assigning blame. Mary Beth turned the tense waiting area in Minneapolis into a gathering of good-humored passengers. She listened to the little voice in her head that said, "I'm the one who can diffuse this conflict. I'm the shortest distance between this chaos and calm." Shortcuts don't add to confusion or tension. Their status, access to information and resources, and their expertise help to lessen it. And it's all made sweeter by a little sugar called humor.

"Yes": Why It's Usually the Right Answer

> The warriors approach to life is to say "yes" to life: "yea" to it all.
>
> —JOSEPH CAMPBELL
> *American author and philosopher*

Michael Kiessig is the general contractor I chose to marshal my home renovation project. He had the most remarkable approach to everything I asked him to do. It was always, "Sure, let me get some information and put some thoughts to that to help you make a decision." It was never, "No, you can't do that; it's not in your budget." His tact was so entirely unlike what I'd experienced before in this realm, where I grew to expect a series of roadblocks and obstacles— the ever-present and, often, presumptuous, "Oh, I wouldn't do that; it's going to cost too much." Or the condescending, "Hmmm, we can't do that. You wouldn't know, but the structure won't hold up."

Not so Michael. His was a Shortcut attitude—a *yes* attitude, a can-do approach. When I asked him if I could vault the ceiling of a particularly long, great room in my home, and open up the back to include the patio, not once did he say what a bad idea it was. He didn't say it would make my house look like a bowling alley or a church hall. Instead, he said, "Let me run some numbers on it, get you some drawings, and then you can make the decision." I did make the decision—not to do it. When Michael presented me with the cost and the picture, I quickly came to the conclusion that it was far too much money to spend to create something that would indeed look like the Monaco Bowling Lanes without the neon lights. Later, by the way, I did learn that Michael knew immediately when I asked for the design change that it would look ridiculous and cost an absurd amount of money. Yes, he helps dissuade clients from making bad decisions; but only after they explore it with him. He's open to the possibility that the client might actually have an idea he hadn't considered, that it might be one that works.

Michael's philosophy is that with enough money and time, the answer is always yes. But let the client decide, not the service provider. That's such a radical yet simple concept. As a Shortcut, Michael provided me with all the information I needed to make a decision. And if I had decided to create the bowling alley effect in my great room, Michael would have accommodated me; but only after offering further insight.

My experience with Michael and his company led to a lot more business for him in our neighborhood, because whenever a neighbor asked me, "Would you recommend your contractor for our renovation?" I answered with a resounding yes! That's the power and influence of an effective Shortcut.

There are may ways you can find to say yes in your own work. More than anything else, it is a habit you can develop. Here again, attitude comes into play, as I explained earlier. Obviously, if you have a pessimistic attitude, and you don't believe you or the universe can conspire to create a yes situation, then you'll have problems with this optimistic approach to life.

I love to watch people interact when they are most stressed. It's very telling. If you can behave well when you're facing difficulty, chances are good that you'll be more effective in your life than someone who lets that same difficulty cause negativity and gloom, as I described in the chapter on emotional intelligence. A great place to witness stressful interactions is—you guessed it—at the airport (so much of my life is spent in this laboratory). I think the airline industry gets a bum rap overall. Yes, there are those gate agents who are not fit to meet the public; and, yes, it sometimes feels as if the ticket agent is mining our life story as he or she busily clacks at the computer keys, silently staring at the screen for several minutes in order to answer a seemingly simply question we posed.

But, in general, if you see what I see, you'll have to admit that those behind the counter in any airport are up against a crowd of passengers who seem to have lost their common sense and graciousness when they entered the facility; and most of those airline professionals do a pretty good job trying to reintroduce sanity to the process.

All of that said, I am particularly interested in observing the back and forth between an airline's top-level "platinum" passengers and the agent at the gate as these travelers work earnestly to get upgraded, finagle a better seat, or win some other favor. On one occasion in Baltimore's airport, I found myself amidst a typical late-afternoon madhouse in the boarding area. I stood near the desk at the gate so that I could do my undercover observation. I watched as two gate agents handled their respective lines of passengers, but in completely different ways, and so with entirely different outcomes.

Agent One told passengers who wanted to change seats that there were only middle seats left, in the back of the airplane. Some of the platinum passengers in that line debated loudly whether what the agent said was true, only to be met with a bit of bad attitude from Agent One (which they undoubtedly provoked with their musings). She said, "Do you *want* me to reassign you to a middle seat?" The less "valued" passengers walked away looking irritated or resigned; but having just watched an obvious travel pro get cut down to size, they weren't about engage in an argument themselves.

Agent Two, in contrast, talked with each passenger as if he or she were a platinum passenger; and when the actual platinum passengers stepped up with their sometimes demanding requests, she handled them as if they were even better than platinum. I watched as passenger after passenger attempted to change their seats. Interestingly enough, Agent Two was able to find some aisle and window seats.

I stood in wonder as I watched the two agents working the same flight. While Agent One consistently asserted there were only a few seats left—and middle ones at that—Agent Two always said, "Let's see what we have open [click, clack]. Okay, it looks like I can get you a few rows closer to the front, but it's a middle seat." The passenger would then usually decide to stay put, but walked away satisfied, having been treated respectfully. And when a premium passenger announced him- or herself as a 100,000-mile flyer, Agent Two would go through the same motions.

Finally, one premium passenger asked Agent Two if she could put him in a different seat, closer to the front. Again she said, "Let's see what we have open right now. Oh, look at that; it looks like someone just decided to stay in sunny Baltimore [it was snowing furiously outside] and that seat has opened up—aisle seat, two rows behind first class. Is that going to do?" What makes this more striking is that Agent One wasn't even looking for those possibilities, with the result that she visibly left people with a bad taste. She wasn't saying yes, on any level. In essence, she was sending the message that it would be more convenient *for her* if everyone would just behave and take the seats they already had.

Agent Two, by comparison, treated the experience as all in a day's work. It probably took her 20 seconds longer to check whether any seats had opened up since the last passenger she spoke with. Often, as it turned out, there were a few new open seats as it got closer to boarding time. At the very least, she left her passengers feeling respected, not like another piece of cargo that had to be loaded on the plane.

Shortcut Lesson

The Shortcut isn't always responsible for making the decision, but he or she is always there to serve as a resource to help the person making the decision. The best Shortcuts have a *yes* attitude and proceed to pull together enough resources and information to help someone else arrive at a decision. They do not only look for information to corroborate their opposition to the idea. And they do not scold requestors into agreement.

You become a better Shortcut by understanding the subtle positive shifts in attitude you can create just by saying yes.

Choices

The Rewards of Offering Them

> For what is the best choice for each individual is the
> highest it is possible for him to achieve.
>
> —ARISTOTLE

One of my clients was a physician who had the expertise part of his job down pat. However, he struggled with the emotional intelligence aspect, and it was beginning to affect his career. He was being considered for partnership in his practice, but he was the subject of a lot of complaints, from both patients and staff, relating to his harsh approach; so I was asked to work with him.

To begin, I asked him to take note of the complaints being made about him and what he thought the complainants' side of the story was. When we met the next time, he had an incident to share. As it turned out, this would be the impetus for a simple shift in his thinking, which would later prove to unlock the secret framing of a Shortcut for him.

I'll call this physician Dr. Smith, and his patient Dianne. Here's how Dr. Smith reported the interaction he had with Dianne, who wanted an expensive and mildly invasive preventative procedure:

Dianne: Dr. Smith, I'd like to get a "scope" because, as you know, this cancer is in my family—my brother and mom—and I'm nervous about it.

Dr. Smith: You are a 30-year-old woman in perfectly good health. There is no indication that you need the scope, because you don't have symptoms and your insurance company isn't going to pay for it if I can't professionally recommend it. And I can't. Sorry, we won't be doing the scope just yet.

Dr. Smith explained to me that he also told Dianne he would not recommend her for the procedure for another 10 years (when it was indicated for someone with family history), unless she became symptomatic sooner.

That incident led to Dr. Smith's being called on the carpet by his practice chief. When I asked how he might have approached the interaction with Dianne differently, to get a different outcome, he was stumped. He asked for my opinion. Here's the conversation I role-played for him:

Dr. Smith: So, Dianne, you're feeling a bit anxious about your family history with this cancer. That's completely understandable. But you should know that your blood work shows you to be in great health, without any indication of cancer. Let me tell you what we're looking at, and then you can make a decision. Right now, you don't present with any symptoms that would warrant the procedure. Basically, your risk for the cancer—even with your family history—doesn't go up significantly for another 10 years. At that time, we can go ahead and do the procedure preventatively.

Probably, your insurance company won't pay for the procedure at this time, and it's relatively expensive—about $3,000. So my recommendation would be to wait until you're 40 to have the procedure; until then, make sure you come visit me for an annual evaluation. Or, if worrying about this is keeping you up at night, and is affecting your ability to enjoy life, certainly you can opt to pay out of pocket for the procedure, and I'll be happy to fully explain to you the risks that are involved with it.

Dr. Smith asked me how I came up with that approach so quickly. I told him, simply, practice. Shortcuts practice behaviors that put control where most people want it: in their own hands. Shortcuts use their considerable expertise and resources to advise, rather than make decisions for others, demand, or pass judgment. A light went on for Dr. Smith. He understood.

Shortcut Lesson

Most of us want to have choices, and most of us also seek advice and maybe a little handholding from a Shortcut to help us decide; but, ultimately, *we* want to be the one who chooses.

The degree to which you, as a Shortcut, can give me well-informed choices is the amount by which your stock as a Shortcut goes up.

Stickiness

The Good and Gooey Ways of a Shortcut

> Anytime you can expand your network and users in this market, it's significant. The goal is to make it "sticky," make users come back to it.
>
> —DAVID SMITH
> *American sculptor explaining the art market*

Steve Saykally is an automobile service representative. At first blush, you might think a title like his would be a conversation-killer at a cocktail party. But you'd be wrong. I'd pit him against any service professional in any industry; I'd also bet, with his Shortcut attitude and approach, he'd come out smelling like a new car every time.

You might say that Steve has a head start as a Shortcut because he works for Cadillac. Cadillac is known for a lot of things, and its service is one of them. Steve is either exceptional because he works for Cadillac; or he works for Cadillac because he's exceptional. Or maybe both. The point is that my interactions with Steve have always been exceptional because he's got the "stickiest" of Shortcut approaches I've experienced anywhere.

Each time a "client" buys a new car from Cadillac, a service rep is assigned to him or her, to stick with the customer for the entire period of ownership. Some Cadillac reps, including Steve, have been with the dealership where I do business for more than 20 years. Every time I get my car serviced there, it is always wonderfully pleasant. My guy Steve makes it that way. If you had my customer experience, I guarantee you'd think twice about getting a different brand of car from a different dealership—all because of Steve's sticky behavior.

For example, it was time for my routine 10,000-mile checkup; I also needed to have a slow-leak tire repaired. I made the appointment online—a nice Shortcut, by the way!—for a day when I could drop off the car early in the morning, have a friend take me to the airport to head out for a two-day business trip, and take a cab back to the dealership to pick up my car when I returned. Here's how my brief conversation with Steve went when I dropped off my car:

"Hey, Scott, how you doing?"

"Great, thanks. Cool online booking system you have now."

"Yeah. We thought it'd be better for you if you could make an appointment any time you wanted instead of having to call in. Glad you like it."

Steve and I went through the items to be checked and fixed on my car. Then Steve noticed my front-end damage. I told him I hadn't had time to have it repaired, and since it didn't get in the way of the performance of the car, it was low on my list of priorities.

Steve said, "So, you're back in a couple of days? If you'd like me to, I'll drive the car over to the collision center [a completely separate business from the Cadillac dealership] and get an estimate for you. I'll leave you a message and let you know what it'll cost. If you decide to go ahead with it, I can make an appointment to have it repaired, if you want to do it sooner than later. Just let me know."

Knock me over with a feather. The guy knows I travel a lot, and, yes, he might be rewarded somehow for getting the repair done; but he is the epitome of a great Shortcut. He takes care of what the client has no time, talent, or inclination to do. But that's not the clincher; that's only partially gooey. Here's the really sticky thing he did, in a matter of 30 seconds:

"So, you have someone dropping you at the airport this morning?" Steve asked casually.

"Yes, I do."

"You said you're coming from the airport to the dealership to pick up your car. How are you going to get here?"

"Cab."

"That's like a $40 to $50 ride. Here are a couple of cab vouchers on us that'll take care of about half of it."

Like glue. Stuck. Steve is constantly thinking about how he can make his clients' lives easier. You might think he's dreaming this stuff up all day, because it flows so easily off his tongue. Or that Cadillac gives the reps all kinds of devices like this to impress its customers. But my hunch is that this is what Steve practices in all aspects of his life. The why and how of it really don't matter; what matters is the result—that I'm more loyal to the brand because of him. He's a Shortcut to me, as well as to Cadillac, because the company doesn't have to reinvent a customer. I'm hooked—or stuck, as it were.

Shortcut Lesson

Steve is an example of sticky. Successful shortcuts *are* sticky. They make their companies piles of money and keep the customers coming back. They create stickiness by doing many small things very well. They also find ways to make every part of every transaction seamless and easy for their clients. They pay attention and think a step ahead; the result is a fully satisfied, greatly impressed, and permanently sticky customer.

Responsibility

If You Take It, You'll Make It

> Let everyone sweep in front of their own door. Then the
> whole world will be clean.
>
> —Johann Wolfgang von Goethe
> *German playwright, poet, and novelist*

Several years ago, when I was working as a television news and
documentary producer, I had the opportunity to interview
death-row inmates for a documentary on capital punishment. After
our first interview, the cameraman, Tom, and I walked out of the
interview room feeling utterly confused. Was the man really guilty?
Based on his side of the story, both Tom and I were having serious
doubts as to whether or not this man had committed the horrible
crime for which he'd been convicted, and was now facing the death
penalty. His account was compelling, his tone convincing.

"So how'd it go?" the warden asked us.

"Uh, fine," I said, "but . . . we both were just wondering if
this guy is maybe, uh, not guilty. His story is so radically different
from what the court records say, and he's so believable. What if he's
locked up for something he didn't do?"

The warden looked at us and chuckled. I thought he was being
callous.

"You've been had," he said, going on to explain that a Bureau of
Prisons statistic at the time suggested that more than 90 percent of all
inmates on death row are convinced they are not responsible for the
actions that put them there. He went on to recount detailed evidence from this man's particular case file that had contributed to

his conviction (the jury had no trouble reaching a verdict). It was hard to argue with facts, but nevertheless Tom and I were stunned. We had no experience with the crime world, and our naivete was showing. I had never been in an environment where no one took responsibility for their actions.

That is until I went to work in the corporate world.

Of course, all companies have their cultures; but I was amazed to see how many employees of large corporations—from the top down—refused to take responsibility for the mood and morale of their workplace; for the way things were going for the company in general; even for their own careers. In my conversations with individuals, I found something that paralleled my conversations with the inmates at the prison: it was always somebody else's fault—*they* made a stupid decision; *they* did the wrong thing; *they* didn't treat people fairly; *they* didn't care about anyone. The implication being: So why should I—do the right thing, treat people fairly, care about others?

Shortcuts, in contrast, take responsibility for their actions and behavior. Perhaps that's why they are the people we want to be around (and why we're willing to pay for their services). They create their own reality, one that works for them.

In her exquisite book, *Bird by Bird: Instructions on Writing and on Life*, Anne Lamott[21] points out some uncanny ironies of life as experienced through her work as a writing professor. Two things she describes are spot-on about our existence on this planet, and even truer of the Shortcut journey.

First, Lamott has noticed over the years that her students all come to her with a desire to be published, but few of them actually want to *write*. In my work with executives around the world, I have noticed the same phenomenon. Most execs want the perks and benefits of being at the top, but not many are willing to do the work it takes to get there. The sacrifices, study, hours of work, and other demands are grueling. It is not for the faint of heart. But then again, that's why Shortcuts become so influential. Most workers aren't willing to do what it takes to become excellent Shortcuts. The most distinguishing factor between the Shortcut and those who only wish to be one is that Shortcuts keep on going.

That's another area I found a parallel between the life of a writer, as described by Lamott, and that of a Shortcut. She says that the process of writing requires that all who do it produce what she so charmingly labels "the shitty first draft." She says no author is exempt from this requirement, no matter what their skill level. Lamott claims that it's a universal law, because when you write that first draft, you write and write and write and write; you write until you want to give up, and then you write some more. And just when you think you've had enough, you get to the forty-eighth page; and there it is, on that forty-eighth page: the *first* page. The only way to get to the first page is to have written all the others. No one escapes that process.

Shortcuts have that same stick-to-it attitude, the tenacity, which enables them to do a few more "pages." In contrast, the Shortcut wannabes don't realize they were just one or two pages from finding their real "first page," because they give up too soon. The Shortcut keeps on "writing."

Shortcut Lesson

Shortcuts take responsibility for all their efforts, even the crummy ones. They are prepared to learn from their "shitty first drafts" and not cast blame on the *theys* of the world.

Feelings

Happiness Is a Warm Shortcut

> Winning isn't everything, but the will to win is everything.
>
> —Vince Lombardi
> *football coach*

All feelings—good or bad—produce a "halo effect." It has long been known that humans are conditioned to assign positive thoughts and feelings to products associated with people we like or admire, who endorse the products. Witness basketball superstar Michael Jordan (Nike, Hanes underwear, McDonald's); actor, singer Queen Latifah (Pizza Hut, Jenny Craig); soccer player David Beckham (Adidas); and actor and model Andie McDowell (Maybelline). They all have, or have had, multimillion-dollar contracts to be the "face" of various products.

B. Zafer Erdogan, a well-known market researcher in the area of celebrity endorsements, has conducted studies that show those millions of dollars companies spend on famous spokespeople are worth every penny.[22] We buy products promoted by famous people because of the feeling we have for the "names," more so than the product—at least initially. The good feeling you have for a celebrity, you transfer to the product he or she is promoting. If the likes of basketball superstars Charles Barkley and Michael Jordan, and actor Kelsey Grammer (*Frasier*) tell us that McDonald's burgers and fries are delicious, well, then, we think, they must be—or they're at least worth trying. The reverse holds true, as well. When a celebrity loses our respect or confidence because of some public disgrace (bad behavior, illegal activity, etc.), very often, he or she subsequently loses their millions in endorsements because companies can't afford to have a negative role model associated with their products. The halo affect, in short, works both ways.

As a Shortcut, the halo effect likewise applies to you and/or your product; that is, the feeling part comes into play. People have a tendency to forget what you say, and they might even forget what you did for them. But they will always remember how they felt when you or your product or service reappears on their radar screen.

One of my favorite times of the year is around November and December. I love the holidays and what they stand for. At the same time, one of my least favorite times of the year is around November and December. I really hate to wrap and send gifts (it's the process of wrapping and going to the post office I hate, not gift-giving itself), but I do it. I know I could go online to shop and ship, but I prefer to send homemade gifts. However, I often procrastinate because I know I'll spend a good deal of time addressing and wrapping the packages so that a jackhammer would have trouble breaking through them. In the past, I would schlep them to the post office and stand in line with all the other late-to-mail shoppers. I don't have anything against the USPS, but, I dreaded the de-holly-jolly feeling I got while standing in a line that wrapped around the block.

Then one year I discovered the Postal Centers USA Store near my house. It's not a post office; it's one of those postal stores. Who knew? They do it all for you. I bring in my gifts, wrapped only in holiday paper, with the address and phone number for each one written on a sticky note. The staff at the Postal Centers USA Store *happily* and *properly* pack each one of my packages for shipping. They weigh each package, add up the total, take my money, and send me on my way. Lines are shorter, people's tempers are longer, and everyone ends up happier. It's the perfect Shortcut for a holiday package sender like me.

Here's the payoff for them and for me: I now do all of my shipping throughout the year from this store. The employees there act as if they know me. They act as if they're happy to see me. Nothing is a hassle to them. I'm never made to feel like an idiot for wanting to ship a television wrapped in duct tape. They just make it work. It *feels* great.

Shortcut Lesson

Shortcuts are a true win/win. Everyone likes to be a winner, and when the Shortcut makes you feel like you win—even when they take your money—that sensation continues long after the Shortcut service is complete. We return over and over again to our Shortcut, even if the rest of what they do is not really out of the ordinary. Now who's the big winner? The Shortcut, once again.

Context

Make Things Right, the Shortcut Way

> Wisdom is your perspective on life, your sense of
> balance, your understanding of how the various parts
> and principles apply and relate to each other. It embraces
> judgment, discernment, comprehension. It is a gestalt,
> or oneness, an integrated wholeness.
>
> —STEVEN R. COVEY
> *author*

One of my favorite Shortcut retail chains is the Container Store. You can find anything in there you need—and many things you don't, really—to organize your life. The employees all seem to have been hired for their love of organization, thus I treat them as on-the-spot Shortcuts when I have a question about storing something or organizing a closet or cupboard.

Once when I was in my area store, waiting patiently up front while the components for a closet I was working on were being gathered, I struck up a casual conversation with the door greeter, in between her directing customers to the areas of the store they needed. (It's all about Shortcuts in that place.) Time passed pleasantly while we talked, until it dawned on her that we had been chatting for some time. She asked me what my last name was, so that she could check on my order. She went to talk to someone with a computer, came back in a few minutes, and said, "You've been waiting 22 minutes, and that's no good; but your order is being assembled right now. We're in the postholiday crush, and our closet sale is going on . . . If you'd like, you can go and grab a cup of coffee; or you could come back tomorrow; or you can stay here and continue our conversation. Whatever you choose to do, it'll probably be another 15 minutes before your order is ready. I apologize for the wait."

Not only is that greeter a Shortcut to shoppers; she is also one for the Container Store. She managed the context of my experience so that the company doesn't have to go out and find new customers all the time. If my experience had been managed otherwise—with indifference, say, or with a "deal-with-it-we're-busy" attitude—I might not go back to that store again, and would probably have bad things to say about it to my friends. Instead, I have become a regular customer, who has nothing but good things to say to everyone I know about this great Shortcut store.

How smart would it be for companies all over the world to manage the context of their customers' experience in similar fashion, thus creating a Shortcut to profit (avoiding bad word-of-mouth, as well as the need to reinvent customers)? Let's face it, most people hate the phone-tree abyss into which they fall when they have a service or technical question. It's time-consuming, and we're usually making the call when we're short on time and already frustrated with the product or service. If I were treated by the phone company, my computer service representatives, software people, or airline reservation staff as I was at the Container Store, I know my ire at being put on hold would be substantially relieved.

Imagine, for example, this conversation with a technical customer support person when she finally connects with you:

"Hello, my name is Kate. I see from my little crystal ball that you've been on hold for over eight minutes. That has to feel like an eternity. I promise to help you with your issue as quickly as possible. If we do get cut off, again, my name again is Kate, and my direct line is . . ."

No doubt you would be disarmed and, perhaps, charmed—and, consequently, become more cooperative and less cranky. You wouldn't spend time brooding or expressing your displeasure, and would therefore get your problem addressed more quickly. In the end, you might at least come away with a neutral feeling for the company you were calling—or even feel positively disposed, even though you waited so long on the phone. All it takes are a few words of acknowledgment. Shortcuts come in many forms; and managing context effectively is, without question, one of the single most valuable things you can do as a Shortcut.

We all know how to manage context, if you think about it. Does the following ring a bell with you? As a teenager, I knew when, who, and how to ask for the car keys. My request was never the same, even though my goal—to borrow the car—was. I had a sixth sense that told me when the parental "units" were predisposed to accommodate my needs. Sometimes I bided my time, waiting for the right moment; and if it didn't come along by the time I needed the keys, I managed the situation to make a yes response more likely. Even though it was a time of life when much of what we did could be dismissed as growing pains, moody phases, and rebellion, most of us learned that million-dollar Shortcut skill, *managing context,* during those years, and we've never forgotten it. We may lose track of it at times, but we can master it again. And by doing so, I assure you, it will change most of your relationships for the better.

Remember this important guideline: *The context in which a request is made predicts its outcome.* The content itself usually does not presage the outcome, unless it's earth-shattering. You might assume this is "just" common sense; but negotiations gone awry and negative business outcomes paint a different picture. (Consider the "eight minutes on hold" scenario I just described.) In my work with executives, on a variety of career paths and at different levels in their organizations, I never cease to be amazed by how many of them think that having something important to say, or needing an answer *right now,* means that it's acceptable to forget that all-important lesson of context. They assume that whatever it is they so desperately need—a person, a service, or information—gives them the right to say what they want, to whomever they want, whenever they feel like it, and however they want.

This is clearly not the case with successful people, in general; and for Shortcuts, the opposite is true. The concept is simple, and has a basis in brain science. The simple part is this: When someone is in a nasty mood, he or she is much less likely to do what you want, even if you are making a reasonable request. Countless salespeople plod through their pitches to clients because they have a standing appointment to do so, or because they have the clients in the room and they don't want to let them get away. Such situations lack impulse control, empathy, and overall awareness. Those who are highly competent in these aspects of emotional intelligence know that sometimes the best meeting is a five-minute chat that replaces the hour-long one they had planned. They survey the landscape before they make their pitch, and *manage the context*, moving it when necessary to a more positive space. Or they decide to put everything on hold until it's better for the client.

Brain science has proven that when we are in a negative frame of mind, experiencing one of the three chief negative emotions—anger, fear, or sadness—we regress to behavior that helps us survive. We are less open to new ideas, and so very often will say no, simply because we want to focus on whatever brought on the negative emotion; we don't want to have to think about anything new or that will interrupt our train of thought. Conversely, when we're feeling positive, we are more likely to collaborate; we become more open to suggestions, and we're a lot more likely to say yes—or at least maybe—to new requests.

Skilled professionals manage the context of each interaction to increase its appeal; and their sales' quotas and general success prove the wisdom of doing so. They know that to push ahead in a negative situation is futile. The steps to manage the context of a situation are not difficult, but they are extremely important. You must:

1. Determine what the mood is. This requires empathy, and an ability to see things through the eyes of anyone else involved.

2. If the mood is negative, ask questions and listen carefully to what you're being told. That said, take care not to interrogate a person in a negative state. He or she will close down even further. Focus your line of questioning on finding out whether you should even be there.

3. Ask, sincerely, if it would be better to reschedule the appointment. If now is the only time the client can and wants to talk, tread lightly, be brief, and speak in high-level bullet points. Remember, the client will be doing little actual listening if he or she is in a bad space.

4. Look for any sign of light in the dark mood and build on it. If a client says he or she likes something, for example, take time to give more information about it. This is your opportunity to get a little chattier, and to bring the context into a more positive place.

5. Once you've maneuvered the context into a more positive position, you can negotiate and sell—but not a moment before.

Shortcut Lesson

When you change the context from negative to positive, you're doing the same thing you did when you negotiated the car keys from mom or dad. You're being smart, emotionally aware, and appropriate—and you'll be more successful. There are the keys; now go out and ask for them.

PART FOUR

The Shortcut as a Company

We aren't happy until you aren't happy.
—*Imagined Mantra of Many Ineffective Companies*

THE SHORTCUT ORGANIZATION

It was one of the most stunning un-Shortcut moments I had witnessed in a long time, the kind that only takes a few seconds but that defines an entire company culture.

I was sitting on a jam-packed airplane, watching the usual goings-on of preflight hustle and bustle. I was fortunate enough to have been upgraded to first class, where the flight attendant up front usually takes passengers' jackets and hangs them. The man across the aisle from me, in the window seat, saw one of the uniformed airline employees walk down the aisle. She happened to be the gate agent, but she was on board. From his seat, he couldn't easily get up and hang his jacket himself without causing commotion. So he asked the ticket agent to please hang his jacket. Her response was remarkable. She recoiled, literally, with a look of disgust, as if to say, "Ewww; don't get that thing near me." What she said, in a tone to match her disgusted look was, "Oh, no. I'm not a flight attendant. I'll get one for you."

With that, she turned abruptly toward the front of the plane, but not before she caught my incredulous look, which said, "Do you need a lesson in how to operate a clothes hanger?!" She knew she was in the wrong, but she proceeded to get the flight attendant who was busy hacking away at a bag of ice.

Those of us in the first two rows caught each others' eyes. This little exchange had been lost on no one. Then I burst out laughing— it was just so absurd, and the perfect illustration of the anti-Shortcut, and what it can do to change the reputation of a company.

Unfortunately, that ticket agent's behavior speaks volumes about the way employees in this company (which shall remain nameless) behave in general. Sure, there are those who work there who wouldn't hesitate to take the man's jacket and hang it. But more times than not, this airline's employees seemed to go out of their way to "educate" customers on just who does what, and for whom. There is no corporate "stream of consciousness," to help customers, no matter the job title of the employee; and the lines of demarcation are many. It comes across as if the employees are angry at their employer and want their customers to feel the same pain. "We aren't happy until you aren't happy" seems to be their motto.

Creating an organizational Shortcut Culture is, to be sure, a major undertaking, but it can be done. The organizations that have already accomplished this shift are notable, and their customers are generous with both praise and loyalty—which translates into revenue. Those who have not, and continue to make missteps like the one just described have a tendency to overlook many of the small things that result in a first-rate customer service reputation. Over time, such companies become yesterday's champions and today's gone-bankrupt news stories.

There are four distinct areas your organization can focus on to create a Shortcut Culture:

- Executive buy-in (from the CEO, COO, CFO—the "C-level" execs) of the need for the Shortcut Culture

- Education of the top 10 percent of senior leaders in the organization, and their subsequent practice of what they've learned

- Education of all employees at all organizational levels

- The hiring process

EXECUTIVE BUY-IN

Many excellent organizational programs fail because those at the very top are aloof about the rest of the company. Consider these two extremes, which I witnessed personally.

- At GE, Six Sigma—the robust process improvement program—flourished, because Jack Welch made it a requirement for all senior leaders to complete the program. They had to become, essentially, "black belts" in the process if they wished to be promoted to the executive ranks at GE.

- At another company, the CEO approached Six Sigma with a lukewarm "we'll see what happens" attitude—"I'll believe it when it actually saves me money."

You know how this played out. At GE, the Six Sigma badge was one of honor and rigor. The employees at all levels made it work. The ruling philosophy there, when managers would rumble that the initiative was losing energy or that it had become passé (as one higher-up put it), was "Good! That means we're finally in the right spot, because the moment that you become bored with it is just when employees are getting with the program." The message was: We're sticking with it, because it works, if you work it.

No organization is going to change overnight; in fact, it will probably take from three to five years before everyone gets swept up in the fervor, and the philosophy becomes corporate culture. Too many C-level executives want that overnight result. But I cannot think of an instance when that happened—at least not in my experience.

Need I report that the company whose CEO demonstrated only lackluster buy-in of the Six Sigma process saw only slim to modest results—and the initiative died from lack of interest within a few years. The people on the front lines take their cues from their managers, who take their cues from their supervisors, who take their cues from the directors, who . . . all the way up to the CEO.

When the CEO at the second company gave the message "I'm not taking this seriously," neither did the employees.

If you're a senior executive and you're reading this, realize that you can't reap the benefits of a Shortcut Culture if you're not willing to walk the talk yourself. Your employees are *not* just listening to what you say; they are *watching* what you do—like a hawk. They will gain energy from your passion and take direction from your behavior, so be careful where you lead them. To create a Shortcut Culture, your employees have to see you "living it" on a daily basis. Keep in mind, "culture" is just a fancy word for "how we do things around here," and it should never be treated as a casual thing. Doing so makes and breaks companies across the globe, every day. CEOs have a very direct impact here; but all too often, they don't realize its importance and so leave it to chance, until those working for them become as confused as the CEO seems to be. And the financial results inevitably tell the tale.

One more thought about corporate culture and executive-level buy-in: We've all heard the adage that employees will treat their customers the way they're treated. It's true. And though you probably don't need a study to prove it, there are many that do, including: "Linking Organizational Characteristics to Employee Attitudes and Behavior," by the Evanston, Illinois-based Forum for People Performance Management & Measurement.[23] The research for the study was conducted by James Oakley, assistant professor of marketing at Purdue University's Krannert School of Management in West Lafayette, Indiana. The Shortcut message of the study? The culture of the organization and the behavior of employees are intimately related. It is cause-and-effect, pure and simple.

I want to conclude this section on a positive note, by describing an organization that embodies the concept of a Shortcut Culture: the world-class Broadmoor Hotel in Colorado Springs. It is, without a doubt, one of the single most beautiful spots you'd ever hope to find yourself in; and the company culture is one where Shortcuts have the opportunity to strut their stuff. I had gone there to speak for an organization that was holding a meeting at the hotel. While setting up the conference room where I would be speaking, I complimented the audiovisual man who was helping me, telling him how much I appreciated how accommodating he was. He helped me rearrange the furniture in the room; he obtained extra supplies for me; and he was patient with me when I changed my mind about the configuration of the room at the last moment—all with a smile. But when he looked somewhat perplexed at my remark, I felt moved to explain to him that this wasn't my typical experience at other hotels; that I usually found myself treading lightly when asking for help or changes. He replied humbly, "I honestly can't imagine what those people think they are there for. You are my one and only concern right now."

That was just the beginning. Over cocktails that night with my group, milling around on an outdoor veranda overlooking Pikes Peak, I made small talk with the bartender. I marveled at what a great spot this must be to be working. He agreed, it was indeed; but then he quickly shifted the conversation back to my experience.

"So, how is it for you here at the Broadmoor? Are you getting everything you need?" Remember, this is the bartender. I assured him I was, and told him how impressed I was that all the staff had been going out of their way to make sure that I wanted for nothing, from the moment I checked in.

To which he said: "I want to tell you a secret." He looked around and lowered his voice as if he might get in trouble if anyone overheard what he was about to say. I was intrigued, and leaned forward.

"You know how the Broadmoor employees treat you here," he continued, "that is exactly how our managers treat us. They make sure we have everything we need and they treat us like we're the most important asset in the place." What a concept.

That's a Shortcut Culture. It's top-down, and it's an entire way of functioning. It doesn't happen by default; it happens by design. You can well imagine that professionals in the hospitality industry might clamor to add the Broadmoor to their resumes. Probably, I could also go back there five years from now and find many of the same employees happily looking after high-paying guests—and doing it all with a sincere smile.

EDUCATION AT THE SENIOR LEVEL

You can't stop with the top, obviously. Educating to build a Shortcut Culture has to continue in a direct line, to the next level; and this is where a company's tactics are going to be critical. Senior-level managers, those just below the top, are usually so overwhelmed and busy, and so badly in need of Shortcuts, that the Shortcut organization needs to institute strategies and rules they can easily adopt and practice.

Every organization is going to be different, of course, but the following credo is a good place to start. Its concepts can be adapted, added to, or subtracted from, as needed. Or they can be used as the foundation from which to formulate entirely new strategies. The main point to keep in mind here is that the organization's highly visible senior-level managers have to be seen implementing these practices on a daily basis.

The credo of the Shortcut Organization:

- Nothing is more important than filling the needs of our customer.

- Every customer of the company is the customer of each of us.

- We are each other's customers, as well.

- We don't have to solve every problem for the customer, but we must find the person who can solve the problem, and then courteously introduce the customer to that individual.

- It is the responsibility of each of us to spend a minimum of 20 hours per year to increase our skills and knowledge. The company will enable this by providing the time and resources to meet this responsibility.

- It is the responsibility of each of us to learn the fundamentals of excellent communication, problem solving, negotiation, and emotional intelligence so that our colleagues and customers benefit from our expertise and positive attitude. The company will provide the resources for up to 10 hours annually to learn and reinforce these skills.

- We will treat each other, regardless of title or station, with the same respect and dignity that we treat our valued customers.

- It is our responsibility to demonstrate our competence at our current job level before we can expect to be promoted.

- We will value our family and private lives in the same way we wish them to value our corporate lives.

These are only a few of the concepts and attitudes that senior managers can exemplify through their consistent behaviors.

One more important point here: In any group setting, you reap what you tolerate. If negative attitudes and mediocre skills are tolerated, this sends the message to all employees that slacking off from the high-level behaviors of a Shortcut is acceptable to management. Over time, the organization as a whole will begin to behave as every other mediocre organization—with confusion, chaos, and, ultimately, failure.

For it to work, senior executives must agree to support a Shortcut Culture, then to start practicing it and advocating it throughout the organization. They must talk about it in meetings and reinforce it with incentives and recognition programs; they should put reminders at the bottom of all internal e-mails and memos, and in internal newsletters. In essence, it must be talked about, acted upon, and rewarded—and then talked about some more. It's not an exercise; it's a way of being.

Any organization that espouses the beliefs of a Shortcut culture will provide a positive and memorable experience for anyone who comes into contact with it. Such was my experience upon walking into the offices of Jobing.com to do an interview for the company web site. This business exudes a persona. Its web site is chock-full of video interviews and articles that help job hunters with job prospects, tips on interviewing, and many other career enhancing bits of information. And on the employer side of the job aisle, it enables member companies to reflect their corporate personalities so that candidates can go to this site and get a real sense of each company culture, to see if it suits them. It's one of the quintessential Shortcuts companies out there.

The same is true in "real life," at the company's regional headquarters in Denver. Imagine an open-plan office, where the cubicles are surrounded by low walls so that everyone can see each other. They are also surrounded by huge windows that overlook downtown Denver and the front range of the Rocky Mountains. That was impressive enough, I thought, when I walked in. Then this happened almost immediately thereafter: Dean, the man who was going to interview me announced loudly, "Say hi to Scott, everyone! He's here to do an interview on emotional intelligence!"

Practically in unison, the entire 20- to 30-something group replied, "Hey Scott; thanks for being here. Way to go—welcome!" To say it was disarming is an understatement. At first, it felt like I was at a fraternity rush party. Then I got caught up in the energy of the room. As we were setting up for the interview, I heard applause and whoops and hollers. It happened several times, at which point Dean noticed the startled look on my face and explained that the employees celebrate every time someone makes a sale.

The Shortcut Culture of Jobing.com and its personality are what separate it from other employment sites. And it passes on that Shortcut sensibility to its clients. Job candidates aren't just seeking a place to make money and receive benefits. They want to work in a place that *feels* good to them as well. They're interested in the personality of the companies they're researching. Jobing.com has figured out how to "bottle" that, and include it on its member companies' profiles. It is an invaluable tool.

I hasten to add that Jobing.com doesn't just do this for its clients, but for its employees, too. They hire for personality and energy. Everyone gets involved. Although the Denver branch manager has an office with a door, when I was there, he was in the bullpen—on the phone, hooting and hollering with the rest of his employees.

Later, when Andrea, the community relations director at Jobing .com, was preparing to walk me out of the building, she hollered out, again to my bewilderment, "Scott's leaving everyone!" To which shouts of "Thanks!" and "see you!" burst out. Those who were on the phone held up those wacky fake hands that clap when you wave them.

I knew I had been in the presence of a Shortcut Culture. I didn't have to guess at what this place was all about. Frankly, I didn't even have to need their services. I was so captivated by the energy, the personality, and the clarity of who they are that I wanted to be a part of it. They created a Shortcut Culture that would take volumes to explain, but only seconds to feel. They do that same thing for their customers so well because they live it.

EDUCATION AT ALL LEVELS

Clearly, it's critical to "infect" the entire company with the Shortcut mentality. It seems like a tall order, and, yes, it will take some time—especially if you're just introducing a Shortcut Culture. However, once people begin to get caught up in the energy generated from experts working with experts, it will gain its own momentum. That said, the bigger your company, the longer it will take. And as with anything, the more energy and effort you focus on it, the more quickly you'll begin to see results.

The employees "in the trenches," who make up the bulk of the company staff, will have to witness senior executives and their direct managers walking the talk on a consistent basis. And, remember, employees respond well to recognition and reward, so it's necessary to identify then compensate Shortcut behaviors and attitudes.

You'll also need to educate employees at all levels if you want to make true Shortcut believers and achievers out of them. Give them the opportunity to attend workshops on emotional intelligence, negotiation, critical thinking, and influence; you want to increase their awareness of what makes others (customers and colleagues alike) tick. Offer training in job-specific skills—or at least provide some resources to encourage workers to do this on their own. You want to raise their expertise levels above those of your competitors. In short, put your company's money where its "mouth" is: support the attitudes and aptitudes you want your employees to exhibit. You also want to encourage loyalty, and offering this kind of employee education is one giant step toward loyalty.

Google is an example of a company that has achieved Shortcut Culture buy-in at all levels. Ask any Google employee what it's like to work there, and you'll hear nothing but pride and see demonstrations of loyalty. This is the direct result of an environment created deliberately by Google management to entice—and enhance—the attitude and aptitude of one of the most famous Shortcuts in modern history: the most widely used Internet search engine. Managers live the "buzz" they want others to pass on about their company; and that buzz makes Google one of the most coveted places to work in the high-technology arena.

THE HIRING PROCESS

The Google buzz extends to its hiring practices, the fourth and final element necessary to create a Shortcut Culture, from the get-go. New hires must *feel* the culture—and feel *good* about it. If you Google Google's hiring practices, you'll learn there are about 100 qualified applicants for every job. While technical proficiency will earn you a ticket to an interview, and is a major success factor at Google, the company also cares a great deal about who you are as a person. Microsoft, GE, and other venerable companies have Shortcut hiring methods as well. In addition to knowledge and skills, they are looking for a "certain something," which they don't necessarily announce to candidates, because they want to be able to find people who come naturally to that "certain something." Each of these companies has a Shortcut Culture and they know who will— and who won't—flourish in it. They are looking for the people who will be a Shortcut in their organizations. They are intent on identifying those who will bring a cooperative synergy to the organization. But that is a moving target, so the hiring process must be dynamic.

It's the same with any relationship. A married couple interacts in one way when it's just the two of them; then their first child is born and the dynamic changes. It has to. Add another and the dynamic changes again. The parenting skills that worked for the first child might not work for the second one, so the family has to adopt new strategies to be successful. The relationship between the parents will have to change, as well. It's the same process in a Shortcut Culture.

Shortcut Cultures institute hiring practices that help them identify those who are not just experts, but who are emotionally intelligent, as well—the two main Shortcut attributes. These companies check references about work habits, put candidates through a battery of aptitude tests and emotional intelligence tests (e.g., the EQ-i, ECI, MSCEIT, etc.); they also ask questions like those given in the Shortcut Quiz in this book. They ask questions seemingly unrelated to the skill aspect of the work, of this sort: "What would you do if . . . ?" "Tell me about a time when you became very angry at work. What did you do?" "If you had to pick only one specific thing that you do that you believe would increase this company's success, what would it be?"

Most importantly, Shortcut Culture companies will include several employees to take part in the interviewing process. These employees are coached to probe for the same qualities but in different ways. These companies are looking for "real" Shortcuts, and consistency is a part of that.

Shortcuts Transform

> I once knew a chap who had a system of just hanging
> the baby on the clothes line to dry and he was greatly
> admired by his fellow citizens for having discovered a
> wonderful innovation on changing a diaper.
>
> —DAMON RUNYON
> *nineteenth-century American journalist and writer*

In regards to creating Shortcuts, all of the same rules apply to corporations that pertain to individuals. If your company is not providing a Shortcut to someone or something, it won't be viable for long. Why do you think companies spend billions of dollars each year in their research and development departments? It's because they have all these really smart people with steam coming out of their ears working on the latest and greatest Shortcuts. Look at some of the things that those steamy inventors created: Post-it notes, Velcro, zip-lock baggies, no-spill sippy-cups, faster computer chips, telephones that tell you who is calling, paperless credit card approval systems, better PDA devices, mess-less toothpaste dispensers, quieter jet engines—and the list goes on and on.

Each of these items was invented and brought to market to create a better Shortcut. Each cost many millions of dollars to get to the consumer. Each pays off handsomely.

If you're charged with the next big thing for your company, pay attention to the things that will lead you to the next transformational Shortcut. Take Apple, for instance. Up until the iPod, the company's computer users were considered to be relatively narrowly niched in areas like graphic art and publishing. Then the iPod came along and organized—transformed—music. The iPhone quickly followed with the next transformation for Apple and the rest of the world. It put billions of dollars into the pockets of Apple share-holders. These two products were *transformational* Shortcuts, not transactional. A transactional Shortcut would be the upgraded release of the 16GB iPhone from the 8GB version. That will make the company some money, but it's not the stuff of legends. The transformational Shortcuts are what make legends.

Apple invented something that existed in pieces. Apple just had the engineering and foresight to put it all together. Apple engineers married a tiny handheld computer with the internet and software, telephone technology was added and all of it came together with an internet store that specializes in entertainment—iTunes. Apple simply watched what was being used out there in its realm and asked, "How can we make this easier for everyone?"

So, how do you follow Apple and help your company make transformational Shortcuts? What Shortcut might your company provide that it's not providing already? Try asking your employees how they use your product themselves. Send out "posses" of people to watch customers. You'll have your next Shortcuts just by seeing the unconventional and unintended ways that customers are using your product. That was the Apple way.

That Shortcut philosophy has brought companies fortunes for a long time. In their book, *If it Ain't Broke . . . BREAK IT!*,[24] authors Robert Kriegel and Louis Patler discuss several companies that empower their people to find better, easier ways to use their products. Levi's, for example, listened very carefully to a group of employees who noticed customers that were doing the strangest thing. They were taking their jeans, running over them with their cars, putting them in the washing machine with a bit of bleach, and then wearing them with these odd, beat-up looking patterns. They looked like really old jeans. Levi's management listened, and they saw an opportunity to create a new Shortcut. They stonewashed the jeans for the teens and created a multimillion-dollar market. Harley Davidson did something similar by adding chrome to its bikes upon witnessing the after-market add-on of the chrome. The Hell's Angels were the catalyst for the trend, and Harley made a very wise and profitable business decision to add the chrome themselves—and provide another Shortcut for its consumers.

Shortcut Lesson

Looking for more revenue streams in your company? What are your customers doing to adapt and customize your products to their specific needs? Do it for them—only better. Shortcuts are excellent at spotting the trends because they are experts in their area. They are *trendsetters* not *trend-getters*.

Shortcut Paradise

The Evidence Is All Around Us

All great masters are chiefly distinguished by the power
of adding a second, a third, and perhaps a fourth step in
a continuous line. Many a man has taken the first step.
With every additional step you enhance immensely the
value of your first.

—RALPH WALDO EMERSON
essayist, philosopher, and poet

While transformational Shortcuts can reap big rewards, there is money to be made in the transactional Shortcut. But if you're going to be or create a transactional Shortcut, take care not to make so slight an improvement that it is deemed unnecessary or, worse, ridiculous.

Consider the *Skymall Catalog*, tucked into the seat pockets on nearly every airplane in North America. It could be the single most thumbed-through magazine in the world. It's filled with all kinds of things you never knew you needed—it's filled with a lot of Shortcuts. Some are highly innovative, others are undoubtedly headed toward an early demise, and still others spark Shortcut ideas for browsers just by looking at them. I, for one, owe my organized closet and laundry room to one of these catalogs. It's popular because it's fun to look at, but also because we are enamored with anything that promises to give us more time, create more mental space in our lives, or help us to have more fun.

Yes, there are hundreds of catalogs like *Skymall*, which are mass-produced and distributed by mail, including *Improvements, Sporty's*

Tool Shop, Brookstone, Frontgate, and oh-so-many more. What's so brilliant about *Skymall* is that someone had the insight to say, "There sure are a lot of Shortcut catalogs out there, and people sure do love to look at them and buy from them. What if we compiled a Shortcut catalog of all the Shortcut catalogs and put it where people are typically bored out of their minds—on airplanes?"

But the lesson here isn't just in the great gizmos that show up on the pages of this catalog. It's in the opportunity customers have while thumbing through the magazine to imagine which things they think will last in the marketplace and which will be short-lived. This exercise can help you in your pursuit to become an invaluable Shortcut, as an individual or an organization.

Case in point: One of the items featured in *Skymall* was a paper towel dispenser that automatically produced exactly one sheet at a time when the user waved his or her hand in front of it. It cost $50. I'll let you decide on the value and need for this product. Another was a space-saving outlet, selling for about 10 bucks. You plug it into your wall outlet and it converts the standard two-plug setup to one with four plug-ins—in essence, giving you room for two more plugs. It also enables you to move furniture up against the outlet without severely bending the cord. How do you assess the value and need for this item?

Shortcut Lesson

It's useful to complete this exercise in regard to yourself—what you offer as a Shortcut. Ask your friends and colleagues about your service or product. Do they need it; and, if so, how much would they be willing to pay for it? If someone were thumbing through a *Shortcut Mall* catalog and came across you and what you have to offer, would they say, "You've got to be kidding me! Is this a joke?" or, "Cool! I need one of those"? Think about it.

Shortcuts Here, There, and Everywhere

> k txt me tomo b4 u do nething wit ur fam. well def hang
> if ima be able 2do sumthin cuz im fo sho chillin idk whr
> tho.
> —Courtesy of Joseph (16) and Sarah (15) Lassen

The epigraph here is a sign that the Shortcut idea has even crept into our language and everyday communication. In this case, it's the XYZ generations that are responsible. It seems they're in such a rush that including vowels in their exchanges gets in the way. Here's the translation of this text:

> Okay, text me tomorrow before you do anything with
> your family. We'll definitely hang out if I'm able to do
> something because I'm most likely going to hang out,
> I don't know where, though.

Wow.

Shortcuts permeate our lives in so many ways. Most of them have to do with trying to save time, no matter what it takes—even if that means dropping vowels. One of the world's largest conventions and trade shows—the Consumer Electronics Show in Las Vegas—is all about promoting the latest Shortcuts. Billions of dollars are spent every year to create the next thing consumers talk about and use—because billions of dollars are made by selling the things that consumers talk about and use. If you look at the new products that techno-guru companies like Microsoft, Apple, Sony, Sun Microsystems, Dell, Hewlett-Packard, Nokia, Motorola, and others are putting out there, you can't help but notice that most of them feature just slight adjustments to their predecessors, offering, at best, minor Shortcuts (the transactional Shortcut I described earlier). Nevertheless, these are minor adjustments for which we're willing to pay. Rarely are these products revolutionary, such as the iPod and GPS automobile navigation systems. They're more the equivalent of a dropped vowel.

Fortunately, you as an individual don't have to spend billions of dollars to make a significant impact as a Shortcut. Look around you, and take note of the things that annoy you. Therein lay the clues to effective ways Shortcuts can delight and offer value to their companies, colleagues, and customers. Most of the time, these are minor in execution but major in impact. You don't have to look for the big splash to make one as a Shortcut.

Here's an example. I was on the phone the other day with a question for my credit card company. As is typical, the first prompt asked me to give my credit card number, the last four digits of my Social Security number, and my zip code. Then I made the selection to get to a "real person." I was pleasantly surprised when a customer service rep came on and said, "I have all the information you've given us already, but I'd like to ask just a few more questions for security purposes." I was surprised because, usually, the CSR asks me to repeat all the information I just gave to the "robot" that answered the phone. This always ticks me off and makes me want to ask, "Why do you have me input all of this information if you are going to ask me to repeat it again anyway?" Many people I talk to are likewise peeved by this by-now common annoyance. It's the companies that pick up on the "little stuff" like this that make us believe they're paying attention to the big stuff as well.

Similarly, when I get on an airplane, if the seat upholstery and carpeting are extremely dirty, and the window shade doesn't go up and down the way it's supposed to, it sure makes me wonder whether the airline is also neglecting to take care of the cockpit controls and the engines on its planes. Doesn't the airline realize that its value proposition goes down because I'm thinking negative things about it? Multiply me by the thousands of others thinking the same thing, and over time, I guarantee, that airline is going to have to spend millions of dollars cleaning up its image, when it would have cost much less to clean the seats and carpets and repair the window shades. Doesn't the airline realize that the billions of dollars it spent building its positive Shortcut image can vanish in a moment? My point is, long-term successful Shortcuts pay attention to the minutiae, to the details. They send the message that they are so good at what they do that they have, and take, the time to put all the pieces—big and small—in place. They also stay aware that their reputation as a Shortcut can be taken away in a flash.

Shortcut Lesson

Transformational Shortcuts,—including new products that revolutionize an industry—are great, but most growth comes in the form of smaller, transactional steps. It's the little things that make a difference—it's the vowels. U2 cn b a gr8 Shtct.

Shortcuts Remember When . . .

> Simplicity, simplicity, simplicity! I say, let your affairs
> be as two or three, and not a hundred or a thousand.
> Instead of a million count half a dozen, and keep your
> accounts on your thumb-nail.
>
> —HENRY DAVID THOREAU
> *essayist and philosopher*

Are you clear about the Shortcut you provide for your company? Remember, the one for which you were hired? It's fine to take on special projects, but if you're doing so at the cost of your originally scheduled program, don't be surprised to find that your boss has hired someone to accomplish the tasks you've been failing to complete. The same caution applies to a company's product. The Oops-I-forgot-what-the-customer-wants-in-the-first-place Hall of Fame is littered with products and services that veered away from the original Shortcut. Remember the notable blunder by Coca-Cola, in 1985, when it introduced New Coke? The company changed the original taste formula of the popular soft drink, upsetting customers in the extreme. Then there was the large sunglasses company that offered a $500 pair of sunglasses with a built-in MP3 player. You have to wonder what that was like while you were driving! And speaking of media in strange places, a major appliance company put a TV in the door of one of its refrigerators. It didn't work, for a lot of reasons; but sometimes we just want the toilet to do what toilets do, not wash the dog, too.

Take a cue from the people at *Frontgate* catalog; they stick with their Shortcut strategy, and make millions doing so. *Frontgate*

targets the high-end home owner, featuring house and lawn fur-
nishings and all of the other items that make a house a mansion.
Most of what is offered in the catalog—with the exception of a few
items—is not significantly different from what is sold elsewhere,
but *Frontgate* banks on the reputation it has built around featuring high-quality, luxury items, as well as traditional products with
a little twist. The buyers for *Frontgate* comb the market for practi-
cal goods that appeal to a consumer with expendable cash, so the
company's products are of slightly elevated quality and workman-
ship, compared to what is found in most other places. *Frontgate*
has established itself as a Shortcut for a distinct market: owners of
"America's Finest Homes." And it is continuously improving and
evolving to find the best ways to satisfy this market.

Shortcut Lesson

Keep your eye on the Shortcut that people want in the first
place. Hone it, add to it, delete from it, polish it up, as
necessary—but do not lose sight of what the *original* Shortcut
is. People are resistant to change; many resist it fiercely. So
although you may be longing to add innovations to your
product offering, be sure first that your customers want those
updates. You may discover they are happy with a product
they have come to know and count on. Stick with a winning
Shortcut, unless you know a change would be welcomed by
your target audience.

PART FIVE

The Long and Shortcut of It

Humility makes great men twice honorable.

—BENJAMIN FRANKLIN

SHORTCUTS ARE EVERYWHERE: FATHER OF THE YEAR

I regard my father as one of the greatest Shortcuts in the universe. But I didn't always, not until I came to understand everything a Shortcut embodies.

In 1977, when I was a junior in high school, the younger half of the seven-person Halford tribe to which I belong wrote a letter to our local newspaper—*The Littleton Independent*—to nominate Dad for the father of the year. And this was our letter:

> Dear Littleton Independent,
>
> We nominate Jim Halford for father of the year. A few things you should know about him are: He doesn't have a big title; he doesn't make very much money; he's not politically active; he doesn't volunteer. He's not a part of the Lions or the Elks or Kiwanis or anything else. He does not give back to the community. He doesn't travel a lot. He doesn't speak very much. And he's not a public figure at all.
>
> But what he does is this: He's at home every single night at 5:00 o'clock, with his beer and his newspaper. And every night when there's something going on in our

lives, there's something going on in his life. And every weekend, when we are playing baseball or softball or tennis or hockey, or there's a play, he's there. At every one of our events, he is there. And he's roaming around and he's running a million miles an hour. And sometimes he's our coach, but mostly he's just our dad.

And we think that's what a father's about. So we think he should be father of the year.

Well, Jim Halford won. We could have told him before the reporter came to interview him for the story, but we opted to wait to see the look on his face when he heard the news. So that night, reporter Garrett Ray came to the house. (We had warned him not to come before 5:02 P.M.—not a minute earlier. We knew Dad needed at least two sips of beer before the "ambush.")

So 5:02 comes, and ding dong goes the doorbell. No one gets up to answer the door. Mind you, our father was not used to answering the phone or the door; he's got a wife and children, and they do that. But none of us gets up to answer the door. The doorbell rings again.

"Somebody get the damn door!," Dad hollers. We look around at each other, knowing who's at the door. Finally, we go to the door, then tell Dad it's for him. Already he's out of his element, because in his mind, nothing but bad news requires his attention at the front door. He gets up with an irritated sigh and goes to the door.

"Mr. Halford, my name's Garrett Ray from *The Littleton Independent*. Your children have nominated you for father of the year. And we are happy to say that you have been selected."

My dad stood there bewildered. Now Garrett says, "Mind if I come in and ask you a few questions?" We could tell that Dad was still not convinced one of us was not in trouble.

We all file into the living room, where the reporter asked Dad a very interesting question (I actually thought it was kind of silly):

"Why is it that you think you won father of the year?" I could see my dad thinking but not saying, "I don't know. I didn't nominate me."

Instead, he sat there for a few minutes; finally, what he said was something very remarkable. He started with my oldest brother, Doug, and went through his seven-child empire, all the way down to my youngest brother, Terry, and talked about what each one of us had accomplished, and what it was about each of us that made him most proud. It was the first time in my life that I had heard my father utter such words. I didn't know he knew me like that. I had no clue. He described his success through our successes.

Dad is an "action" Shortcut; he lives by the principles of one. His tacit creed as he nurtured each of us to adulthood was: "I measure my success after I measure yours. If I can see how you are, I can see how I am. It's not that I take on your identity. It's not that your self-worth is my self-worth. It's that if I helped you and you got to where you want to be, then I've done what I'm here for."

After the reporter left we sat down for dinner. Everyone was quiet. It reminded me of Christmas morning, after all the gifts have been opened and everybody's thinking, "Okay, what now?"

Dad didn't say anything. But I remember my mom made soup that night; and the reason that I remember it is because my dad was huddled over his bowl, like someone was going to steal it from him. In reality, he was attempting to hide, because for the very first time in my life, my father was weeping in front of us.

Later, upon talking it over with my siblings, we all agreed that our surprise hadn't produced quite the "ta-da" we had hoped it would. But in retrospect, I realize Dad was so moved and humbled by the fact that his family, and then the newspaper, would recognize him for something he thought was his "job" that he couldn't express himself. I could almost hear him thinking: "This is why I'm here. All my life, this is what I've worked for. It's just what I do. And you think it's great? I never knew."

Shortcuts seldom recognize that their everyday efforts are often experienced by others so dramatically—almost heroic, at times.

Thus, they may be surprised by the accolades that come their way. Dad could have been rich; he could have been a lot of different things, because he's extraordinarily talented and smart. What he became is a Shortcut in the lives of me and my siblings. His job is father; that's what he decided would be the focus for his life. That's what he chose.

Shortcut Lesson

Shortcuts appear in all walks of life and at every level of a hierarchy. You don't have to have a fancy title and make a lot of money to be a Shortcut. You can be one right where you are today.

The Lessons of the Shortcut Have Always Been There

Wisdom is the right use of knowledge. To know is not to be wise. Many men know a great deal, and are all the greater fools for it. There is no fool so great a fool as a knowing fool. But to know how to use knowledge is to have wisdom.

—CHARLES H. SPURGEON
nineteenth-century English preacher

Several years ago, in preparation for a keynote presentation to a large group of end-stage cancer patients, I interviewed a number of people who were facing the final six months or so of their lives. Since none of them had anything to lose and all had come to peace with their mortality, they all had the uncanny ability to wade through the noise and chaos of "trying to become successful," in which most of us nearly drown.

What I learned from them changed me. Their lessons were of the magnitude that social scientists, performance experts, and psychologists have long worked to quantify, measure, and verbalize. The scientists call it "emotional intelligence" and "wisdom," and explain it with research and statistical analysis. These people, in contrast, *demonstrated* it, with eloquence, candor, and insight, which comes only from deep reflection—which many of us are too busy "living our lives" to indulge in.

I fully expected to feel gloomy, scared, and a little low after meeting these people. Instead, I felt energized. When I finished my conversations with them, I felt as though I needed to hurry up and start living, implementing the lessons they'd taught me. I didn't need to face my own death to begin. That's the first thing I learned.

One of these people, a woman named Phyllis, explained how her good friend Sue would come to visit her. Though Sue was very intelligent, she was also snide and cynical about the world. Phyllis noticed that after every visit from Sue she felt drained, and would need to take a nap. "Other people would visit me," Phyllis said, "sometimes while I was feeling particularly lousy, and I'd find the energy to walk a couple of laps around the block with them."

Then she said to me: "Scott, you're healthy, but the same thing is happening to you. People come into your life everyday and either take or give energy. You do the same thing, too. We don't notice it as much when we're healthy, but when your immune system is as battered as mine, every bit of energy is felt for what it is."

Being a Shortcut is about the positive or negative energy you choose to bring to every situation. Those with emotional intelligence *choose* the positive. Emotionally intelligent living requires a mindful effort; and it's the more difficult part of being a Shortcut. If you don't want to read all the studies of emotional intelligence, simply ask yourself this Shortcut question: Do people feel good or bad when they are with you? Do they feel like they have to take a nap after you leave? Or do you make them feel invigorated enough to go out and take a walk? Whichever reaction you evoke in others, it's due to the energy—good and bad—that you emit. Shortcuts are aware of theirs, and opt for the positive.

Another of the patients, Steve, described himself as a nonemotive, quiet chemical engineer. "If I could do it over again," he said, "I would have more courage to speak up. I would sit down and go knee-to-knee with the people who matter most to me, and have conversations that are real, authentic, based on the truth. Those are tough, I know, because I avoided them. And now I have them, and it's not as scary as I thought. It works so much better for everyone. It feels so much better. I feel like I'm going to die an honest man. That really seems to matter now."

The ability to have deep, intimate conversations with family members, friends, and coworkers is one of authenticity and honesty. Shortcuts live their lives with integrity. If they're competing, it's with themselves and external elements. They know that the only way to become an indispensable Shortcut is to be honest about what they can and cannot do. They "get real" about their strengths and talents, and then get busy working on the ones they do have.

All of the end-stage cancer patients with whom I spoke proclaimed the importance of simplicity. One person in particular stated that we are so busy trying to live the easy life that we only succeed in making it complex. "The greatest comfort," she said wistfully, "is getting back to basics—finding peace in the small things, because that's all I have energy and time for—the small things. And that seems to be just right."

Shortcuts bring simplicity to life. They notice the small things and take care of them. They delight in the seemingly mundane, and bring a sense of awe to all who witness their joyful approach to those small things. They make others come to life.

Phyllis said it beautifully: "You know, I think I knew this stuff all along. It's kind of like a secret that we all know at heart. I didn't take the time to slow down, get quiet, and understand that life is about as wonderful and successful as we make it—for other people."

Shortcut Lesson

The Shortcut proposition is simple:

Get Shortcuts. It's the single easiest thing you can do to make your life more enjoyable and your success more attainable. Find experts and use them!

Be a Shortcut. You write your own ticket when you focus on mastering a service or product and then offering it with positive energy and a good dose of emotional intelligence.

Enjoy the process. Life is sweet because of the journey we choose to take, not because we get to the end of it.

As Dr. Seuss said, "Don't cry because it's over. Smile because it happened."

Epilogue

Some Things for Which There Are No Shortcuts

- Happiness

- Love

- A life worth living

- For most of us, getting rich

- A really good, healthy body

- Nurturing a child to adulthood

- The truth

Appendix: Shortcut Quiz Answers

The answers to the SQI given in the Introduction, along with the explanations for each, are detailed here, along with the related areas that determine a Shortcut:

- Expertise

- Emotional intelligence (attitude)

- Responsibility

- Initiative

Note

You may also take the SQI online at www.BeAShortcut.com.

1. *a., Initiative and Responsibility:* This shows that you take responsibility for your future, and you don't leave your success to fate.

2. *b., Emotional Intelligence (EI):* People who are happy (an emotional intelligence attribute) have a lot more zest; and even when they are tired, they still feel gratitude.

3. *a., Expertise:* If you're viewed as a resource, you probably have greater expertise than most.

4. *b., Initiative, Expertise, Responsibility:* This question, though brief, is fully loaded. If you're not being challenged to think, your expertise is probably not growing. It takes both initiative and responsibility to put yourself into a challenging job.

5. *b., Expertise, Initiative:* The earlier in your career you can choose a path of expertise that works for you, the more quickly you will become the go-to resource. It takes initiative to change careers when your current one feels like it's not right for you.

6. *a., Initiative, Responsibility, Expertise:* It's your responsibility, and it takes your initiative, to educate yourself. Shortcuts are committed to their own growth.

7. *b., Emotional Intelligence:* It takes assertiveness, stress management, reality testing, and problem-solving (all EI attributes) to delegate when you're anxious. Shortcuts know they are not at their best when they're feeling stressed, so they lean on their Shortcut network to help out.

8. *a., Emotional Intelligence, Expertise:* Happiness, self-actualization, and stress management are EI attributes that work well together; and they can bring about joy and elation, even when a job is quite challenging and you've mastered aspects of it.

9. *a., Emotional Intelligence, Initiative:* It takes many EI attributes to be able to have a civilized, timely discussion with someone when you're angry. Letting things blow over rarely works in the long run. The issues behind the anger just fester and can become explosive if not dealt with properly. Shortcuts don't let bad feelings slow things down. They take care of problems promptly.

10. *b., Emotional Intelligence, Initiative, Responsibility:* The first answer, doing it with a smile, is passive-aggressive and does not really get at the heart of the matter. Shortcuts don't carry a lot of emotional baggage around with them. To be an excellent Shortcut, you must take responsibility for your own success; that requires taking the initiative to have a difficult discussion and the EI to conduct it in a productive way.

11. *b., Emotional Intelligence, Expertise:* The first answer is vengeful, and leads only to further bad feelings. The correct answer, b., shows you to be an assertive and clear resource.

12. *a., Emotional Intelligence, Initiative:* It takes courage to speak up about difficult issues, especially when they feel personal to you. Again, Shortcuts do not allow emotional baggage to sabotage relationships. They deal with things head-on.

13. *b., Expertise, Emotional Intelligence:* When you are at your best in challenging and stressful situations, time will pass quickly because you are busy solving problems and dealing with issues. Shortcuts who are in "flow" lose track of time.

14. *b., Expertise, Emotional Intelligence, Responsibility:* You're a Shortcut if you don't subject others to your prioritization process. The question is, can you help or not? Excuses and a reading of your to-do list just waste the time of others.

15. *a., Initiative, Responsibility, Emotional Intelligence:* Shortcuts nurture their networks. They take the steps necessary to remain in contact. Also, people with social networks are more likely to be happier.

16. *b., Expertise, Emotional Intelligence:* While competition can determine a clear winner, and is necessary in many situations, it is collaboration that "bakes" the biggest "pie" in the long run. Collaboration is a win/win scenario. But it takes good negotiation skills to be able to collaborate effectively.

17. *b., Responsibility, Emotional Intelligence:* Awareness is crucial to successful relationships. When a relationship with an individual or a group falters, responsible people look to themselves first to ascertain their part in the situation.

18. *b., Expertise, Emotional Intelligence:* This can be argued both ways, but the success chips are stacked more heavily on the side of a person with emotional rather than financial wealth.

19. *b., Expertise, Initiative, Responsibility:* Another loaded scenario. Answer a. could work, but it borders on feeling as if you're putting your boss in her place. Remember, Shortcuts are resources, and if they don't have the expertise, they find someone who does.

20. *a., Expertise, Initiative:* Shortcuts add value and their expertise. They don't just check off items on their to-do lists.

21. *a., Expertise, Emotional Intelligence:* You may actually be a Shortcut in a career that you're not completely satisfied with; however, odds are that you'll be a better one if you're in a career that excites you. If you're not, by all means, find one that does.

22. *b., Emotional Intelligence, Responsibility, Initiative:* If you "teach" the client who, other than you, to talk to, you're shirking responsibility—dumping the problem back in the client's lap. Shortcuts solve problems; they do not pass them off.

23. *a., Emotional Intelligence, Responsibility, Initiative:* See answer 22.

24. *b., Initiative, Emotional Intelligence:* Sometimes, we back ourselves into corners and get results we did not anticipate. Making someone else "pay" for that is not the way of a Shortcut. Also, an emotionally aware individual is capable of having a discussion to "set things straight" or clarify a point without putting another individual in his or her place.

25. *b., Emotional Intelligence, Initiative:* Everyone responds well to favors. Shortcuts provide them, and then often find favors returned, exponentially. It's the way the world works.

26. *b., Expertise, Emotional Intelligence:* Experts don't have all the answers, but they know a lot of people who do. Also, harboring resentment because you "always have to do it all yourself" brings on a negative attitude, and then you're no longer a Shortcut, no matter how smart or good you are.

27. *a., Initiative, Responsibility, Emotional Intelligence:* Effective people take the time to blow off steam; they also give themselves downtime. Excellent Shortcuts nurture themselves so they can nurture others.

Scoring

21–27 correct answers: You're probably an excellent Shortcut.

14–20 correct answers: You're most likely a very good Shortcut.

7–13 correct answers: You're about average as a Shortcut.

0–6 correct answers: You will benefit greatly from the lessons described in this book.

References

1. Schwarz, Barry. *The Paradox of Choice: Why Less is More* (New York: Ecco, 2003).

2. Cialdini, Robert. *Influence: The Psychology of Persuasion* (New York: HarperCollins Business Essentials, 2006).

3. ———. *Influence: Science and Practice* (New York: Allyn & Bacon, 2001).

4. Milgram, Stanley. *Obedience to Authority: An Experimental View* (New York: HarperCollins, 1974).

5. Naisbitt, John, and Patricia Aburdene. *Megatrends 2000* (New York: William Morrow and Company, 1990).

6. Welch, Jack, and John A. Byrne. *Jack: Straight from the Gut* (New York: Business Plus, 2001).

7. Drucker, Peter. *The Essential Drucker: The Best of 60 Years of Peter Drucker's Essential Writings on Management* (New York: HarperCollins, 2001).

8. de Vries, Manfred F. R. Kets. *The Leader on the Couch: A Clinical Approach to Changing People and Organizations* (John Wiley & Sons, Inc., 2006).

9. Langer, Ellen. *The Power of Mindful Learning* (Cambridge: Da Capo Press, 1998).

10. Peterson, Christopher, and Martin E. P. Seligman. *Character Strengths and Virtues: A Handbook and Classification* (New York: Oxford University Press, 2004).

11. Buckingham, Marcus, and Donald Clifton. *Now, Discover Your Strength* (New York: The Free Press, 2001).

12. Csikszentmihalyi, Mihaly. *Flow: The Psychology of Optimal Experience* (New York: Harper Perennial, 1991), p. 74.

13. Yerkes, R. M., and J. D. Dodson. "The Relation of Strength of Stimulus to Rapidity of Habit Formation." *Journal of Comparative Neurology and Psychology* 1S: (1908), 459–482.

14. Pink, Daniel H. *A Whole New Mind* (New York: Riverhead Books, 2005).

15. Fisher, Roger, and Daniel Shapiro. *Beyond Reason: Using Emotions to Negotiate* (New York: Viking Penguin, 2005).

16. Bar-On, Reuven. *EQ-i BarOn Emotional Quotient Inventory Technical Manual* (Toronto: Multi-Health Systems, Inc., 1999), p. 1.

17. Plutchik, Robert. *Emotions and Life: Perspectives from Psychology, Biology, and Evolution* (Washington, DC: American Psychology Association, 2002).

18. McClelland, David. *Human Motivation* (New York: Scott Foresman and Co., 1983).

19. Herzberg, Frederick. "One More Time: How Do You Motivate Employees?" *Harvard Business Review Business Classics: Fifteen Key Concepts for Managerial Success* (January 2003): pp. 13–27.

20. Seligman, Martin E. P. *Authentic Happiness: Using the New Positive Psychology to Realize Your Potential for Lasting Fulfillment* (New York: Free Press, 2002).

21. Lamott, Anne. *Bird by Bird: Instructions on Writing and on Life* (New York: Pantheon, 1994).

22. Erdogan, B. Zafer, Michael J. Baker, and Stephen Tagg. "Selecting Celebrity Endorsers: The Practitioner's Perspective," *The Journal of Advertising Research* (May 2001): pp. 39–48.

23. Oakley, James. Linking Organizational Characteristics to Employee Attitude and Behavior—A Look at the Downstream Effects on Market Response & Financial Performance. Forum for People Performance Management & Measurement, Northwestern University, 2005.

24. Kriegel, Robert, and Louis Patler. *If It Ain't Broke . . . BREAK IT!* (New York: Little, Brown and Company, 1991).

Bibliography

Brooks, Geraldine. *People of the Book* (New York: Viking Press, 2008).

Covey, Steven R. *7 Habits of Highly Effective People* (New York: Free Press, 2004).

Covey, Steven M. R *The Speed of Trust: The One Thing That Changes Everything* (New York: Free Press, 2006).

Csikszentmihalyi, Mihaly. *Finding Flow: The Psychology of Engagement with Everyday Life* (New York: Basic Books, 1997).

Goleman, Daniel. *Emotional Intelligence: Why It Can Matter More Than IQ* (New York: Bantam, 1995).

———. *Social Intelligence: The New Science of Human Relationships* (New York: Bantam Dell, 2006).

Sanders, Tim. *The Likeability Factor: How to Boost Your L-Factor and Achieve Your Life's Dreams* (New York: Crown, 2005).

Stein, Steven J. *Make Your Workplace Great: The 7 Keys to an Emotionally Intelligent Organization* (San Francisco: Jossey-Bass, 2007).

Stein, Steven J., and Howard E. Book. *The EQ Edge: Emotional Intelligence and Your Success* (San Francisco: Jossey-Bass, 2006).

About the Author

Scott Halford, CSP, Founder and President of Complete Intelligence, LLC, is known internationally as a substantive and engaging speaker and educator. He is an Emmy Award–winning writer and producer and a long-time consultant to Fortune 500 executive teams. His expertise and experience enrich the contribution he makes to every client situation. Scott's talent in focusing on the strategy and application of concepts distinguishes his work and earns praise from executives around the world. His expansive knowledge in the areas of emotional intelligence, critical thinking, and influence add richness and depth to his programs.

Scott is also known for the insight he brings to the human experience at many levels and in many different situations, and for his ability to communicate in workshops and keynote addresses with humor, wit, and depth. He is a captivating storyteller, capable of transporting his audiences in imaginative ways. Participants of his workshops laugh as they learn, and consistently praise the experience as rich and rewarding, one that has a positive impact on their future success.

Scott is certified in several emotional intelligence instruments including the EQ-i, the Emotional Competency Inventory (ECI), and the Mayer Salovaey Caruso Emotional Intelligence Test (MSCEIT). He is also a Certified Associate in *Emergenetics,* the study of performance and preferences based on genes and the environment, and a Certified Speaking Professional (CSP), the highest earned designation of the National Speakers Association and International Federation of Professional Speakers.

To obtain a Shortcut to programs on Shortcuts, emotional intelligence, critical thinking, and presentation skills, please contact Scott at: scott@completeintelligence.com; or call him toll-free at 800-586-8760.

Be sure to visit www.BeAShortcut.com to take the Shortcut Quotient Inventory and to learn more about all kinds of Shortcuts.

Index

Abilities. *See* Skills

Accessibility of information, 44–46, 89–90

Achievement, 66–73, 155

Acknowledgment, 14, 50, 147, 150, 179–181. *See also* Recognition

"Action" Shortcuts, 209

Adler, Deborah, 91

Advertising, 30

Albright, Herm, 139

Amazon.com, 46

Anxiety, 75–80, 86, 92–93, 150–151, 167–169

Apple, 46, 197–198

Aquino, Corazon, 157

Aristotle, 167

Arthritis Foundation, 109–111

Assertion, 57

Attitude:
  choices and, 167–169
  company culture and, 185–195
  context and, 179–183
  emotional intelligence and, 139, 145–152
  high maintenance employees and, 12–15
  humor and, 161–162
  motivation and, 155
  personal issues and, 25–26
  positive, 139–143, 152, 176–178, 212
  tenacious, 174–175
  value and, 22–23
  "yes," 163–166

Attractor behaviors, 145–152

Audience, status with, 123–125

Authority, 31–33, 109

Back-room activities, 47–50

Bar-On, Reuven, 144

Behavior. *See also* Attitude
  accepting responsibility and, 173–175
  attitude and, 139–143, 163–166
  attractor *versus* repeller, 145–152
  changing, 81–88
  company culture and, 185–195
  context and, 179–183
  humor and, 161–162
  likeability and, 116–121
  positive energy and, 212

"Better" tactics, 39

Billings, Josh, 11

Blame, 162, 175

Boredom, 76–78

Bossidy, Larry, 144

Bottlenecks, 16–17, 27–28, 133–134

Brain, 81–88

Brauer, Nancy, 135–136

Broadmoor Hotel, 188–190
Brooks, Geraldine, 65
Buckingham, Marcus, 67–68

Calling, 159
Campbell, Joseph, 163
Career, 158–159
Celebrity endorsements, 176–177
CEOs (chief executive officers),
    187–190
Challenges, 75–80
Chanel, Coco, 53
Change:
    of behavior, 81–88
    of company culture, 185–195
    value of, 205–206
Chaos, 46, 65–73, 161–162, 191
Chesterton, G. K., 104
Chief executive officers, 187–190
Choices. *See also* Decision making
    authority and, 31–32
    context and, 179–183
    likeability and, 117
    rewards of offering, 167–169
    Shortcut analysis of, 8–9
    social proof and, 29–30
    titles and, 32
Churchill, Winston, 61
Cialdini, Robert, 30, 115
Clifton, Donald, 67–68
Coaches, 80, 87. *See also* Education
Collaboration, 147
Colleagues, 12–13, 125–127, 146–148
Communication. *See also*
    Negotiations; Presentations
    education in, 191
    effectiveness of, 104–106
    with employees, 23–26, 185–195
    honest, 212–213
    influence and, 109, 112
    with network of Shortcuts, 131–138
    shortcuts in, 202

Company culture, 185–195
Competence, 38–39. *See also* Skills
Complexity, 10, 213
Conceptual thought, 99–100
Confidence, 56–57
Conflict, 125–129, 146–152,
    161–162, 164–166
Consistency, 205–206
Container Store, 179–180
Context, 179–183
Cooperation, 118
Cornetta, Mark, 132
Cost, 2, 18–23, 26, 40
Courage, 57, 212
Covey, Steven R., 179
Creativity, 96–97. *See also* Innovation
Critical thinking, 99–100
Csikszentmihalyi, Mihaly, 74–76
Culture, company, 185–195
Customer service:
    attitude and, 140–143, 163–166
    company culture and, 185–195
    context and, 179–183
    emotional intelligence and,
        149–151
    offering choices and, 167–169
    positive feelings and, 176–178
    rules and, 61–64
    stickiness in, 170–172

Dahms, June, 52
D'Aniello, Jacob and Susan, 51
da Vinci, Leonardo, 58
Decision making, 30, 117, 163–169,
    179–183. *See also* Choices
Dennis, Patti, 101
Denver International Airport, 16–17
Desire, 3, 5, 51–52, 83–88, 171
Details, 202–204
De Vries, Manfred F. R. Kets, 55
Diminishing returns, 13, 24, 92–93
Distractions, 58–60, 65–73, 79

Dobens, Lloyd, 153
DoodyCalls, 51
Doubt. *See* Self-doubt
Drucker, Peter, 41
Due diligence, 112

"Easier" tactics, 38–39, 41–43, 172
Education, 80, 87, 190–194
Effectiveness, 6, 8, 37–43, 104–106
Efficiency, 3, 8, 41–43
Effort, 70–71, 174–175
Einstein, Albert, 90
Emerson, Ralph Waldo, 200
Emotional intelligence. *See also*
   Feelings
  attitude and, 139
  company culture and, 195
  context and, 182–183
  education in, 191
  positive *versus* negative energy and,
   212
  relationships and, 144–152
Employee relations, 23–26, 185–195,
   198–199. *See also* Colleagues
Energy, positive *versus* negative, 212
Enjoyment, 71–72, 74–80, 159. *See
   also* Happiness
Erdogan, B. Zafer, 176
Executives, 187–190. *See also*
   Management
Expectations, meeting, 16–18
Experience, 89–95, 108–109
Expertise:
  attitude *versus,* 139–143
  behavior change and, 83–88
  building blocks of, 101–103
  communicating effectively about,
   104–106
  company culture and, 195
  development of, 65–73, 87–88,
   174–175, 190–191, 194
  identifying, 55–57, 68

insight and, 94–95
optimal performance and, 74–80
Shortcuts and, 2–6, 20–23, 171
status shift and, 123–130

Family life, 25–26, 191, 207–210
Feelings. *See also* Emotional
   intelligence; *specific feelings (i.e.,
   happiness)*
  acknowledgment of, 147, 150
  company culture and, 192–193
  context and, 179–183
  positive *versus* negative, 176–178,
   212
Fisher, Roger, 127
Flow (optimal performance), 74–80
Forum for People Performance
   Management & Measurement,
   188
Franklin, Benjamin, 207
Fraud syndrome, 55, 79–80
Friedenberg, Edgar Z., 65
Frontgate catalog, 205–206
Front-room activities, 47–50

Gandhi, Mohandas, 74, 123
Geek Squad, 140–141
Gifts, 70–71. *See also* Strengths
Goals, 84–88
Goethe, Johann Wolfgang von, 173
Google, 46, 194
Gratitude, 6, 150. *See also* Recognition
Guilt, 7

Habit, 84–88, 164, 191
Halford, Jim, 207–210
Halo effect, 176–178
Happiness, 71–72, 74–80, 159,
   176–178
Harley Davidson, 198–199
Heisenberg, Werner Karl, 55
Herzberg, Frederick, 154–155

High maintenance employees, 11–15, 22–23
High value marks, 19–20, 26
Highway I-25, 27–28
Hillman, Anne, 131
Hiring process, 194–195
Honesty, 213
Hubbard, Elbert, 161
Humor, 161–162
Huxley, Aldous, 81

Image, 204. *See also* Self-image
Impostor syndrome, 55, 79–80
Influence:
    attitude and, 23
    authority and, 31–33, 109
    likeability and, 115–121, 176–177
    nurturing Shortcuts and, 133–134
    self-image enforcement and, 125–126
    of Shortcuts, 4–5
    social proof and, 30
    trust and, 107–114, 135–136
    value of, 72, 107–114
Information:
    for decision making, 163–169
    effective presentation of, 104–106
    insight *versus,* 89–90
    mastery of, 66–73
    organization of, 44–46
Innovation, 39, 90–95, 197–201
Insight, 89–95
Integrity, 213
Internal motivation, 155–156
Inventions, 197–199. *See also* Innovation
iPhone, 197–198
iPod, 197
iTunes, 46

Jobing.com, 192–193
Job performance. *See* Performance
Jobs, 157–158
Jordan, Michael, 83

Kiessig, Michael, 163–164
Kriegel, Robert, 198
Kyle, Patricia, 37

Lamott, Anne, 174–175
Langer, Ellen, 63
Lassen, Joseph and Sarah, 202
Lassen, Marty, 111–112, 119
Layoffs, 11–12
Levi's, 198
Library of Congress, 45
Likeability, 115–121, 176–177
LinkedIn.com, 134–135
Lombardi, Vince, 176
Lowest value marks, 21–22, 26
Low maintenance employees, 14
Loyalty, 18, 170–172, 186, 194

MacLaine, Shirley, 51
Maintenance-seekers, 155–156
Management, 11–14, 23–26, 39–40, 187–195
Mastery, 65–73, 104–106, 123–130. *See also* Expertise
McClelland, David, 154
McLuhan, Marshall, 47
Meaning, 157–160
Meetings, 127–129. *See also* Negotiations
Michel, Sarah, 133–134
Middle value marks, 20–21, 26
Milgram, Stanley, 31–32
Mission, 160
Money. *See also* Cost
    company culture development and, 194
    management success and, 40

meaning *versus,* 157–160
motivation and, 154–156
Shortcuts and, 4–6, 10
transactional Shortcuts and,
  200–201
transformational Shortcuts and,
  197–199
value and, 72
Motivation, 153–156
Multitasking, 10

Naisbitt, John, 44
Need, 18–23, 26, 99–100,
  200–201
Negotiations, 72–73, 127–128,
  181–183, 191
Network of Shortcuts, 131–138
Neutral zone, 20–21, 26
Niche services, 21, 51–52
Nightingale, Earl, 96
Nordstrom, 141–142

Oakley, James, 188
Ogden, Roger, 58–59
Oppenheim, James, 7
Optimal performance (flow),
  74–80
Optimism, 163–166
Options. *See* Choices
Organic growth, 91–92
Organization, 44–46
Outsourcing, 47–50

Pascal, Blaise, 35
Passion, 159–160
Patler, Louis, 198
Performance:
  company culture and, 185–195
  in current position, 101–103
  of high maintenance employees,
    11–15
  optimal, 74–80

of original Shortcuts, 205–206
  rehabilitation of, 23–26
  sustaining valuable, 53–54
Persistence, 174–175
Personal life, 25–26, 191
Personal shoppers, 9
Persuasion, 107–114
Peterson, Christopher, 67
Physical attractiveness, 117
Pink, Daniel, 90
Plutchik, Robert, 148
Policies, spirit *versus* letter of, 61–64
Pollard, William, 44
Postal Centers USA Store,
  177–178
Power of Shortcuts, 4–5. *See also*
  Influence
Preferences, 3, 51–52. *See also* Desire
Presentations, 37–40, 104–106,
  123–125
Price. *See* Cost; Money
Prioritization of responsibilities,
  47–50
Process improvements, 41–43, 187
Proposals. *See* Presentations

Quality, 2, 8, 10, 39–40, 206
Qubein, Nido, 1

Ratings, 19–23, 26
Ray, Garrett, 208
Recognition:
  in company culture, 191, 194
  emotional intelligence and,
    147, 150
  likeability and, 118
  of mastery/skills, 55–57, 65–73
  as motivator, 155
  of Shortcuts, 50, 131–138,
    209–210
  as trust builder, 109
  of value, 14

Rehabilitation of performance, 23–26
Relationships:
    with colleagues, 12–13, 125–127,
       146–148
    context and, 181
    emotional intelligence and,
       144–152
    influence and, 107–114
    likeability and, 115–121
    nurturing, 131–138
    self-image and, 125–127
Repeller behaviors, 145–152
Repetition, 82–88, 94
Reputations:
    company culture and, 186
    damage to, 16–17
    details and, 204
    for quality, 206
    rehabilitation of, 23–26
    of Shortcuts, 1–2
    status shifts and, 124
    sustaining, 53–54, 92
Respect, 166, 191
Responsibility(ies):
    accepting, 173–175
    blame *versus,* 162, 175
    focus on current, 101–103
    as motivator, 155
    prioritization of, 47–50
Retailers, 46. *See also* specific retailers
    by name
Rogers, Will, 27
Rohn, Jim, 29
Rubin, Edgar, 99
Rules, spirit versus letter of,
    61–64
Rumi, Jalal ad-Din, 98
Runyon, Damon, 197

Sanborn, Mark, 157
Sanders, Tim, 115
Saykally, Steve, 170–172

Schwarz, Barry, 9
Self-awareness, 55–57
Self-doubt, 55, 74, 79–80
Self-image, 119–121, 125–127, 152,
    209–210
Seligman, Martin E. P., 67, 157
Senior managers, 190–193. *See also*
    Management
Shapiro, Daniel, 127
Similarity, 117–118
Simplicity, 96–97, 213
Six Sigma, 41, 187
Skills:
    attitude *versus,* 139–143
    behavior change and, 83–88
    building blocks of, 101–103
    communicating effectively about,
       104–106
    company culture and, 195
    development of, 65–73, 87–88,
       174–175, 190–191, 194
    high maintenance *versus,* 12–14
    identifying, 55–57, 68
    insight and, 94–95
    meaningful work and, 159
    optimal performance and, 74–80
    Shortcuts and, 2–6, 20–23, 171
    status shift and, 123–130
Skymall Catalog, 200–201
Smith, David, 170
Social proof, 29–30
Specialties, 21, 51–52
Spurgeon, Charles H., 211
Star ratings, 19–23, 26
Status shift, 123–130
Stickiness, 170–172
Strengths, 55–57, 65–73, 157, 159.
    See also Skills
Subordinates, 12–13. *See also*
    Colleagues
Success, 19–23, 26, 39–40, 209
Supply chain management, 42–43

Talent. See Expertise; Mastery; Skills
Technology, 10, 44–46
Tenacity, 174–175
Thatcher, Margaret, 18
Thoreau, Henry David, 205
Time:
  for company culture change, 187,
    193
  context and, 180–183
  high maintenance employees and,
    22–23
  influence and, 108–109, 112
  saving, 30–33, 41–43,
    47–50, 202
  Shortcuts and, 5, 171
Titles, 32
Tracy, Cara, 66–67
Training/trainers, 80, 87, 190–194
Transactional Shortcuts, 198,
  200–204
Transformational Shortcuts, 197–199
Trust, 18, 39–40, 107–114, 135–136

Uniform of authority, 31–32
Usefulness, 58–60, 90–95

Value:
  attitude and, 22–23
  of change, 205–206
  competence and, 38–39
  cost *versus*, 18–23, 26
  high maintenance *versus*, 11–15
  of honest communication, 212–213
  of influence, 72, 107–114
  of insight, 89–95
  of likeability, 115–121, 176–177
  money and, 72
  need *versus*, 18–23, 26
  of positive attitude, 139–143, 152
  of presentations, 37–40
  of recognition, 14
  of Shortcuts, 2–6
  sustaining, 53–54
  of transactional Shortcuts, 200–201
  usefulness and, 58–60
Volume, 19–23, 26

Wagner, Dr., 69–70
Waitley, Dennis, 89
Weaknesses, 68–69
Welch, Jack, 42, 47, 187
Wilson, Warren, 16
Work, meaningful, 157–160

Yerkes-Dodson Law, 78–79, 92–93
"Yes" attitude, 163–166

Ziglar, Zig, 107